Happy gardening!
Don Jacobs

This book is dedicated to Dr. John Freeman of Auburn University.

His long devotion to Trilliums has furnished the foundation for much research on these

AMERICAN TREASURES

Design by Christie Dobson and Jeff Piotrowski.

Printed in USA by Adams Lithographing.

Published by
Eco-Gardens
P.O. Box 1227
Decatur, GA 30031

ISBN 0-9658353-0-8

Trilliums in Woodland and Garden

American Treasures

Don L. Jacobs, Ph.D., Ecology
Rob L. Jacobs, Forest Ecology

Across our land, where pristine woods occur,

Where egocentric humans seldom trod,

Vast drifts of diverse Trilliums abound;

May so it be eternally!

Sans triplet-lilies, could Spring be Spring?

Would Robins sing without their prompting?

Does your heart still race at the viewing?

May so it be eternally!

To know that such drama renews

each Spring,

In unspoiled woods, where Robins sing,

Is comforting, until a mall appears,

And runoff sweeps what the bulldozer clears.

By planning from knowledge we

can preserve,

But it is not enough just to conserve,

We must try to enhance our

shrinking World;

May so it be eternally!

TRILLIUMS IN WOODLAND AND GARDEN

Table of Contents

ACKNOWLEDGMENTS

For one reason, or another, countless persons can rightfully claim input to this work. From Clara and her brother, Tad, whose Trillium Trail bathing site was bordered by lush stands of Trilliums, and whose directions led to more, to the early field botanists, whose records furnished valuable distribution and habitat data, this book has evolved. In more recent time, conservationists, admirers of native plants, gardeners, and nurserymen have pressured us to bring them this publication, and thus have supplied the impetus.

A few noteworthy contributors are no longer among us. A gaping void was created by the loss of Dr. David Vesall in Minnesota. Still young at heart and in years, David's enthusiasm and generosity are legendary. He, and wife Jean, supplied photos of *Trillium nivale* in southern Minnesota. Their gardens at White Bear Lake are inspiring.

Valuable specimens and information have been supplied by individuals from far and near:

Hermann Fuchs and Christoph Ruby, Hof, Germany

Richard Fraser and Art Guppy, British Columbia

Dr. Henrik Zetterlund and Karl-Otto Zita, Sweden

Dr. G. Gusman, Belgium

Matt Bishop, England, furnished photos of *Trillium ovatum* 'Barbara Walsh'

Kath Dryden, England

Dr. Carl Denton has been very helpful in supplying data from British gardens.

Edith Dusek has been very generous with her vast experience with western Trilliums.

John Gyer in New Jersey has reported on his detailed Trillium studies.

Dr. Larry Mellichamp at the University of North Carolina has generously shared plants and data.

Lyle Nordstrom, formerly of Michigan, now of Georgia, is a long-time student of Trilliums who has shared specimens and observations.

Karen Partlow, Mississippi

Wayne Womack, Louisiana

The Georgia Gang: Steve Bowling, Henning von Schmelling, Jim Rodgers, Clyde Rushin, Jim Allison, and especially Tom Patrick of the Georgia Department of Natural Resources, whose continued support is greatly appreciated.

Dr. James McClements of Delaware has never failed to share information, specimens, and excellent photographs.

Dr. Richard Lighty and Mrs. Lammot Dupont Copeland of Mt. Cuba in Delaware have been encouraging and generous with their time in reviewing the manuscript.

All photographs and drawings, not otherwise credited, are the work of the authors.

Those contibutors whose names do not appear here in print, are nevertheless firmly imprinted in our memories. Our wives, Maria and Ginny, have suffered Trillium-time neglect good-naturedly.

A special Thank You! goes to daughter-sister, Kathy, whose flying-fingers computerized this work.

Gratefully,
Rob & Don

INTRODUCTION

Having grown up in the Big Woods of southeastern Minnesota, where winters are cold, summers are hot, and Spring is more than a division of the calendar, a deep sense of vernal rejuvenation has patterned my life. Is it any wonder that Trilliums have taken a place among the harbingers of Spring, and inspired a life-long admiration? They have become inseperably intertwined with concepts of conservation, and subconciously studied in any field work involving woodlands. As an instructor at Summer Camps, as a leader on wildlife field trips, and as a University teacher of Plant Geography and Field Ecology, Trilliums have been part of my

T. catesbaei 'Eco Giant Rose'

consciousness during a long life. For some thirty years, much of my effort has been directed at developing a wide range of habitats on six acres of woodland near Atlanta, Georgia. I call this "Eco-Gardens", for obvious reasons. Vast collections of plants have been established here for research. The emphasis has been on North American and Asian natives. From the beginning, introductions have been carefully screened for superior qualities, and the best have been propagated and assigned cultivar names prefixed by "Eco", such as *Trillium cuneatum* 'Eco Silver Tiara'. As rapidly as possible, these cultivars are made available to commercial nurseries, botanical gardens, and collectors throughout the World so as to insure their perpetuation.

Several hundred cultivars have thus been introduced. Among the best known is *Lysimachia congestiflora* 'Eco Dark Satin', which I selected from my 1983 collections on Mt. Emei in Sechuan, China. This floriferous, prostrate plant was previously unknown outside China, but has become abundantly available throughout North America, Europe, Australia, and elsewhere. Regrettably, the name has been corrupted by some. Since I place no restictions on propagation, and demand no royalties for my cultivars, such corruption is inexcusable.

In more recent time, Son Rob, coauthor of this work, and his wife, Maria, have established Eco-Gardens II in a wooded ravine traversed by a babbling brook, just north of Atlanta. With a degree in Forest Ecology, Rob has been employed to make field surveys throughout the United States. In Eco-Gardens II, he has been something of a purist. He has concentrated on American woodland natives, and his colonies of Gay-wings (*Polygala paucifolia*), rainbow of Mertensias, and Trilliums draw deep sighs from visitors.

Those of us who were born with a compelling curiosity about our natural world can never stop asking why? how? where? And those who zero in on plants will continue to record observations as we photograph and collect seeds and plants. To us plants do not occur as species in the wild. They occur as unique individuals. It is disturbing to realize that the most outstanding are likely to parish, unfulfilled. Survival in the wild is hit and miss. Some kinds are so overwhelmingly successful that they swamp nearly everything near them, but the very uniqueness of an indivdual almost guarantees its demise. While rambling through a beech grove in France in the Fall of 1979, I was shocked to find that the gleeful pigs, snorting and grubbing there, were gobbling Cyclamen tubers. My local companion said, "Why not? There are plenty to go around". In truth, they were more abundant than dandelions in a neglected lawn. Then I saw the finest red one disappear, and I groaned.

Some of us feel a mission to discover and perpetuate the fullness of nature. It would not occur to me to sell one of my recently-discovered treasures, but to propagate it, and to distribute the offspring, brings genuine satisfaction. Further, to use it in a breeding program offers endless possibilities. Herein lies true richness !

CHAPTER 1

ON THE TRILLIUM TRAIL

"Hi you guys! going to the creek? There's a better trail off to the right." A young boy advised Rob and me as we met in a Tennessee woodland. When we continued on our course, young Tad blurted out, "But you can't go that way. My sister, Clara, is bathing in the creek. Hey, Clara, company!" We slowed our pace so Clara could dress. More sinister, is confronting bearded gentlemen toting shotguns while the scent of corn mash fills the afternoon air.

Displaying cameras, and asking questions about native plants, usually converts confrontation into cooperation, and sometimes leads to outstanding discoveries of plants and rural knowledge. Perhaps the very fine *Trillium cuneatum* 'Eco Dappled Lemon' owed its husbandry to proximity to such a still

Despite thoughtfull planning, no plant explorer can hope to anticipate the hardships or pleasures to be encountered when setting forth on seldom-traversed trails. But we have always returned with memorable experiences that made the trek worthwhile. Those who are self-pampered, or faint of heart, may venture forth but once.

Being plants of vernal woodlands, Trilliums may often be enjoyed on warm sunny days, with music from migrating warblers, spritely feeding among unfolding tree leaves above. One such day was not so warm when we decided to cross a pass in the Siskiyous of Oregon. It was mid April, and snowing lightly as we ascended. Snow increased, and soon our low-slung car had become a snow plow. Suddenly our progress halted - a rock had punctured a tire. After mounting the limited-use-donut spare, we were obliged to descend and navigate around the mountain. Happily, such experiences are usually followed by very gratifying discoveries as repayment for perseverance. In this instance, the reward was wonderful, cherub-like, pink *T. rivale* with a pleasing fragrance.

The treeless, rocky hills, treacherous winding roads, and cold mid-April air of eastern Oregon are hardly conducive to pleasant travel, but big purple *Sisyrinchium douglasii* bells, huge yellow Balsamorhiza daisies, and meadowlarks calling across the prairie, lifts the soul of any naturalist. Climax this with descent into moister, Douglas Fir-Ponderosa pine woodland, along mountain streams, and the spirits jump once more. Here in deep, black humus, among grasses, are clumps of plantain-like leaves. *Trillium petiolatum*, a very untrillium-like trillium thrives here in company with gaudy yellow *Erythronium grandiflorum*, false-

7

solomon's-seal, buttercups, meadowrue, and violets. The Trillium flowers are usually nestled at ground level, with the long-stalked leaves held above them. Non-flowering individuals may raise stems six inches or more above the litters, and have shorter petioles. This strange maverick has long been separated by time and distance from its eastern and western relatives. No other sessile Trillium shares its habitat, and (as we discovered) with good reason.

We collected a few select specimens for propagation. The following morning, as our car warmed up, a stench like that from a dead lizard permeated the air. It completely overpowered the wonderful perfume from *Trillium albidum* that had been greeting our mornings. Never-the-less, few Trillium habitats are more fascinating. Regal Steller's Jays call from the stream-side alders. Seemingly-out-of-place, robins probe for worms among the trilliums, elk and mule-deer roam the forest, and clumps of Trilliums pushing through dung piles look particularly lush.

On a cool Spring day in mid April, Rob examined an emerging colony of *Trillium recurvatum* in southeastern Wisconsin. Two weeks later he returned to take photographs. After a disappointing, fruitless search, he discovered only clipped stalks. Every one, of thousands of Trilliums had been consumed by deer. Unfortunately, this is an annual occurrence in many Trillium habitats. It helps to explain why Trilliums in some suburban sites persist more luxuriantly than in many rural sites. Throughout our country, wildlife populations have become greatly out of balance due to activities of civilization. Deer, in particular, have increased to disastrous population levels in most of our woodlands.

A remarkably diverse population of *Trillium cuneatum* was located in suburban Atlanta in 1990. It had survey stakes running

Calypso bulbosa, Mt. Hood, Oregon

through it. Eight very different clones were selected for garden evaluation, and propagation. Revisited in 1994, a strip mall occupied the site.

On one occasion we were advised in mid December of an imminent road cut through a prime Trillium site in rocky terrain. With trowels, small shovels, and freezing fingers, we probed for *Trillium rhizomes*. The following Spring arrived with anticipation, and excitement, as the diversity revealed the fruit of our labors.

On another occasion a torrential Spring storm sent us scurrying for cover in a deserted shack. To our shagrin, another tenant preceded us. It took more than rain to remove the Spotted Skunk's scent - Field work can be tedious, but it is never boring.

There, of course, is no substitute for keen sight when conducting field research, but experience develops all the senses so that a sixth sense evolves, producing a "feeling" for certain things, when in their presence, but before they are seen. On one occasion, a captivating fragrance permeated the forest air. It conjured up images of little Calypso orchid flowers; and there, scattered among showy *Trillium ovatum* plants were the exquisite Fairy slippers. Since then, on several occasions, Calypso perfume has preceded the sighting of both plants.

In nature, scent is a powerful factor. Among animals, it can bring mating partners together, mark territory to keep antagonists apart, warn prey of the presence of predators, and lead to food. Among plants, it may determine success or failure in pollination and seed dispersal. Many examples are demonstrable in which parallel evolution has proceeded between flower structure, fragrance, and pollinating insects, birds, or bats. The volatile oils associated with fragrance are so potent that infinitesimal amounts suspended in air are detectable by human olfactory glands, and many insects and mammals can detect much weaker concentrations. Plants are efficient, not wasteful in most matters, so it should not be surprising to find that perfumes are released only when pistils are ready to receive pollen, and cease soon after fertilization is

accomplished in many plants. Plants pollinated by day-flying insects are often scentless at night, and fragrant in daylight above 50° F, when bees become active. Some flowers with long, slender tubes are scentless in daylight, but turn lose their perfume like clockwork, precisely as darkness arrives, and night-feeding moths with long nectar-sippers take wing.

Some Trilliums have little, if any, fragrance. Some have subtle fragrances that can vary with time of day, temperature, and stage of flowering. Only a few have truly potent fragrances, that are detected long before the nose meats the flower. Two most outstanding examples are both sessile - flowered species. *Trillium albidum* of Pacific Northwest forest margins emits the glorious perfume of Tea Roses, when touched by morning sun and temperatures rising above 50°F. It attracts honey-seeking bees. Under similar circumstances, *Trillium petiolatum* emits a horrible stench that attracts swarms of carion-flies. I have detected no consistent fragrance in *T. grandiflorum*, *T. pusillum*, or *T. nivale*, but the western stalked species, *T. ovatum* (minty), and *T. rivale* (elderberry) usually emit a delicate fragrances. Other Trillium fragrances will be dealt with in the species descriptions.

Is it surprising, therefore, that dealing analytically with fragrances in nature has met with variable success? It is too important to be ignored, and too personal to be scientifically precise. Many plants have been christened by taxonomists with the degrading name "foetid" (stinking). One example, *Iris foetdissima* (most stinking) is the delightful, evergreen, Gladwyn Iris, a plant which elicits no stink whatsoever to me. Serissa foetida, a neat evergreen Japanese shrub has no stink about it. Yet, some of the most vile-smelling plants travel, without warning, in sophisticated horticultural society. Anyone mistakingly by planting the attractive, evergreen member of the Tea Family, *Eurya japonica*, near the entrance to a home, has lived to regret it. As the late-winter, tiny flowers open they emit an overpowering, nauseating stink of a rotting rodent. Only by careful study of the participants, can we fully appreciate the drama unfolding in nature or in a garden.

Erythronium howellii a companion of *Trillium rivale* in the Siskiyou mountains.

CHAPTER 2

THE WORLD OF TRILLIUMS AND PEOPLE

The mind of man can comprehend only the hard-won facts encompassed by his experience either direct or vicarious. Beyond that, he is prone to speculate, and thereby expand his understanding, although it will always be grossly incomplete. It is not surprising, therefore, that a deep reverence inevitably accompanies the contemplation of his awesome World; a world that is formidable, and at the same time amazingly benevolent. It is warm, but not too warn; it is brightly lighted, but the rays are filtered; it is bathed in rains, but they come intermittently; it is surrounded by atmosphere rich in life-supporting oxygen, but not so rich as to burn all life on it; it has sufficient carbon dioxide to support the food factories of green plants, but not so much as would suffocate plants and animals alike. Vast caldrons of destruction boil around the globe, but for each there are antidotes at work to neutralize them.

Think for a moment of the unique properties of water, the molder of our planet, the essence of life on it. It has a most unique temperature - density curve. As it cools, it shrinks, finally becoming heaviest near $+5°$ centigrade, and then reverses and expands, as it cools to become ice which floats on the warmer, denser, water below. If water continued to condense as it cooled to freezing, our lakes would freeze from the bottom up, fish would have no moderate temperature, deep-water retreat - think of how our world would be changed.

Wonderful as our World is, we can abuse her to death. We must study her more diligently. We must learn to support her self-correcting devices, not interfere with, or overload them, or we are all doomed. She has survived horrendous devastations in her five billion years of existence, but only in recent time has man's power risen to threaten his own destiny.

CHAPTER 3

WHENCE CAME TRILLIUMS?

In this context we will consider the Trilliums of the world and whence they came. From beginning, the Earth's surface has been changing dramatically due to natural phenomena. Mountains have risen, and eroded away. Seas have risen to cover large areas of land, and then receded. Great rivers have built extensive new lands at their deltas. And even continents continue to shift about, creating new configurations, new eruptions, and climatic shifts. Under these natural vicissitudes Trilliums arose, migrated about, and diversified. From their simple beginning, they apparently expanded their territory to eventually occupy most deciduous-woodland habitats from the Atlantic Coast of North America to the North Pacific coast, and across the Beringia causeway to Siberia, Korea, Japan, and China, as far as the Himalayas, but not beyond. Much of this extended territory was subsequently lost, and some of it regained. Sometimes the regained territory was apparently occupied by new genetic entities, uniquely adapted to the new habitats. - Now enter modern Man: Plant habitats are not just changing; they are vanishing rapidly.

Trilliums have never been part of the European Flora, nor have they ever occupied the Southern Hemisphere. They are among a

Distribution of the genus Trillium
(includes 47 taxa)

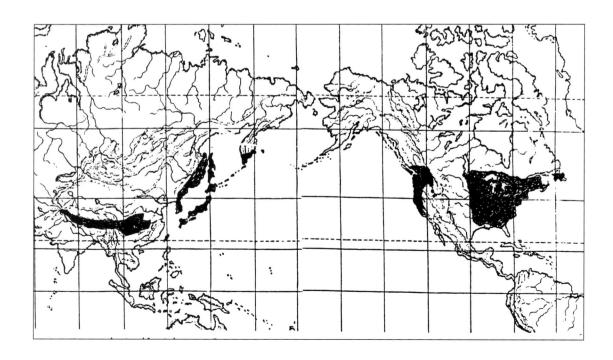

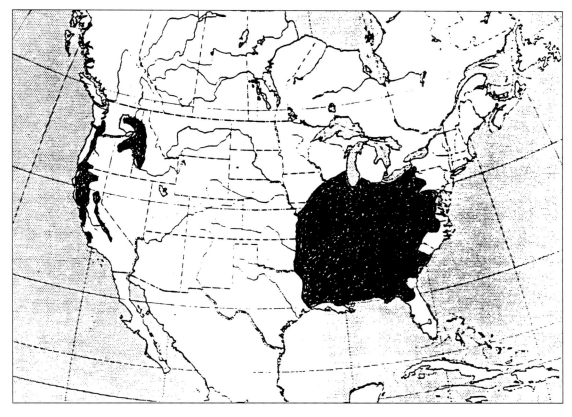

Combined ranges of 23 species of sessile Trilliums. None are known outside of North America.

great number of genera of plants represented in East Asia and temperate North America, but nowhere else. During the past several million years, the two floras have been kept isolated by submergence of Beringia, and by extensive glaciation. Despite the long separation between Asian and American entities the differences are modest.

Trilliums probably came into being during the rapid evolution of flowering plants after the devastastation that closed out the Cretaceous Period some, 65 million years ago. The Appalachians, once taller than the present Rockies, had eroded to perhaps half their maximum height, and the Rockies, and western ranges were only beginning to rise. Vast changes in the Earth's topography, and climate

were occurring then, and continued until recent time. As western mountains rose they presented barriers to the warm, moist Pacific winds heading eastward across the continent. The moist, temperate interior became desert, scrubland, or prairie as the mountain slopes stole the moisture, leaving a dripping coastal band of fog-forest of gigantic trees. By then, the great hordes of dinosaurs had all vanished. A great catastrophe befell our planet; probably a large meteor collision in the Gulf of Mexico, that raised a long-lasting, dense, Earth-enshrouding cloud, resulting in devastating climatic changes, and exterminating all dinosaurs, as well as many other animals in the oceans, and on land, as well as terminating many plants. From that time forward the Earth has experienced alternating periods of cool-moist glaciation, warm-dry, warm-moist, etc. Throughout this extended period of time, only the southern Appalachian region of North America has remained hospitable to plants. The great continental ice sheets of the Pleistocene reached their greatest southward extensions about 25 thousand years ago, and have since been retreating as the climate has become warmer and dryer. The eastern ice sheets stopped at about the Ohio River Valley, and New Jersey, so the Southern Appalachians were never threatened.

The historical distribution of Trilliums is closely allied with the deciduous forest complex. The triplet lilies are characteristic

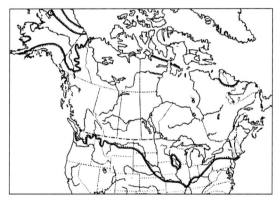

Approximate extent of maximum glaciation in North America during the Pleistocene.

members of the Spring scene in temperate deciduous forests. They typically begin growth when sunlight and moisture are abundant, before tree leaves have fully expanded. As mature tree leaves block most of the light, and transpiration decimates the soil moisture, Trilliums pack up till Fall, having already ripened their seeds. Few Trilliums enter conifer forests, although some may flourish along the margins. Likewise, they are not, prairie or tundra, or desert plants, but some venturesome species, at the margins of their ranges, tolerate

evergreen-chaparral, scrub communities, and even rocky mountain slopes, in order to persist. Such is the case with *Trillium govanianum* in the far-flung reaches of the Himalayas at 9-12,000 feet. Such also is the case with the American West Coast Trilliums that were obliged to adapt, when their rich lowland forest habitats broke up, and pushed skyward, as the mountains rose.

Taxonomists usually deal with Trilliums as a very concise group in the Lily Family, Liliaceae. In fact, it is so neat and concise a group, that some have proposed the family, Trilliaceae, to include them and a very few similar genera, and one botanist placed them in a strange catch - all family, Convallariaceae, Lily of the Valley Family. We can only speculate on the nature of Trillium ancestors, and Trilliums are so current, that the few similar relatives probably arose from extinct Trillium ancestors, but not directly from present Trillium species. The most similar living relatives are about 20 species identified in the genus Paris.

As to the site of evolution of early Trilliums, overwhelming evidence points to the forested coves of the Southern Appalachians.

1. The land mass has remained stable for at least 200 million years.
2. Plant and animal communities have maintained a consistent character as they evolved for the last 100 million years, at least.
3. By far, the largest number of species of Trilliums exist there today.
4. The likely parents of more recently derived species have ranges overlapping in that area.
5. Both sessile and stalk-flowered species are well represented.
6. The greatest genetic variation within species occurs there.

14

7. The least dependence on precise habitat is apparent. Flood-plains, upland, and rocky slopes are occupied by Trilliums.

From their origin in southeastern North America Trilliums diversified as they migrated north and west. Apparently, only a pedunculate type reached what is now Alaska early on. Perhaps the oldest pedunculate Trillium was of the *Trillium grandiflorum* complex. As known today, this is a variable species with the widest range of all. Combined with *T. ovatum*, its western counterpart, the complex once had a coast to coast range that became interrupted by the rise of the Rockies, and subsequent desiccation of the plains. The northern populations were eliminated by glaciation. During the 10-12 thousand years since retreating glaciers uncovered their former territory, much of it has been repopulated, but the eastern and western populations are still isolated from each other. *T. grandiflorum* occurs from our East Coast to Kansas, and from Georgia to Quebec. *T. ovatum* occurs from southern California to Vancouver, British Columbia, Alberta, Montana, and Wyoming. But of great interest are the relict populations remaining in the Colorado Rockies.

From the Alaskan upland, a single early pedunculate Trillium population apparently migrated over the, then exposed, temperate forest causeway, Beringia, and diversified as it gradually occupied Kamchatka, Eastern Siberia to the Amur Valley, Sakkalin island, and south to Korea. Several variants evolved, and occupied the Japanese Islands and the Kuriles. At least one form found its way to the distant Himalayas. The eastern Himalayan Trilliums are the western representatives of *Trillium tschonoskii* which is scattered across central China, Korea, Taiwan, Japan, and southern Sakkalin. All of these asiatic entities are pedunculate. Of the six species and several natural hybrids present in Asia, only *T. kamtschaticum* retains the primitive diploid chromosome number of 10, which is also characteristic of all American species. Other Asian Trilliums have 2N chromosome numbers of 15, 20, or 30.

So far, we have considered only the pedunculate Trilliums. There are nearly equal numbers of kinds of sessile-flowered and pedunculate-flowered Trilliums recognized presently (23+ sessile, 22+ pedunculate). The differences between them are greater than the mere presence or absence of a supporting flower stalk. As a group, the sessile Trilliums have a more restricted range, entirely within the United States. Of the 23 species, 17 are found only east of the Great Plains. The remaining 6 occur only from central California through Oregon to Washington, and western Idaho. There is considerable confusion in recognition of species within the sessile-flowered group. This may be due partly to the early, and continued over-emphasis of the sessile character, stifling the recognition of other diagnostic features. Virtually all of these taxa were at one time identified as Trillium sessile. As currently recognized, *Trillium cuneatum* is probably the most versatile sessile species. It has a lage range, radiating from the southern Appalachian center, in the unglaciated region, and is probably closest to the ancestral type. Several sessile types are probably youthful species, with very limited ranges in the, still young, Mississippi Delta region. The most extensive range is held by *T. sessile* and is mostly within the glaciated area south of the Great Lakes, but extending from eastern Virginia to eastern Kansas. It probably represents a postglacial success story.

The western sessile Trilliums probably evolved from an early eastern migrant close to

15

T. cuneatum in character. In fact, selected large specimens of *T. cuneatum* and *T. kurabayashii* are difficult to distinguish. The other western populations are excellent examples of speciation resulting from isolation of populations during mountain-forming. *T. angustipatalum* is a less robust, narrow-petaled *T. kurabayashii*. The most extreme western variant is the long-petioled *T. petiolatum* with a stem that barely tops the ground litter, round leaves on four-inch petioles spread above the litter, from where the purple sessile flower perches. The plant is admirably adapted to the rugged habitat it has invaded. In the arid transition of eastern Washington and Oregon, across into Idaho strong, dry, cold winds, and bright sun exposure would probably eliminate other Trilliums with elongate stems, and exposed flowers and fruits.

CHAPTER 4

VISIBLE FEATURES OF TRILLIUMS

Were it not for the almost universal recognition of the group of plants we know as Trilliums, Wake Robins, Toadshades, or Triplet-Lilies, we could scarcely have proceeded this far before describing our subjects. They are so simple and uniform in structure, that it often comes as a surprise when their diversity is discovered. Actually, they offer great potential to the plant breeder, and greater potential to the gardener, and landscape designer.

The name Trillium comes from the Greek for three, and no name could be more appropriate. Adult individuals produce no basal foliage, only a whorl of 3 leaves at the stem summit. Furthermore, all floral parts are in whorls of three: 3 sepals, 3 petals, 2 whorls of 3 stamens, and 3 seed-bearing carpels joined into a single pistil with 3 pollen-receptor stigmas. In some Lily-family members, such as Tulips the name tepals has replaced the names sepals and petals, because they are nearly indistinguishable. In Trilliums this is unnecessary. Sepals are the outer, protective members of the flower bud. They are firm and green, but in some individuals they may be suffused with purple. Petals are showy insect attractors. In pedunculate Trilliums, petals are most commonly white, sometimes with reddish markings, or maturing to pink, or entirely maroon-purple. Very rarely yellowish or beige petals are encoutered. Sessile Trilliums are most commonly maroon-red-purple, but virtually all species also produce greenish or yellow individuals, and a few species (*T. luteum* and *T. discolor*) produce

only yellow flowers. Except for the Western *T. albidum*, *T. parviflorum*, and *T. chloropetalum*, white-flowered sessile Trilliums are rarely encountered.

Trillium stamens have rather large anthers with large, sticky pollen that may be yellow, white, gray or purple. There may be as few as 60,000 grains in a *Trillium apetalon* flower, or 1/2 million in *T. flexipes* or *T. cuneatum*. The anthers consist of a pair of long tubes which split lengthwise to release the pollen. The splits may face inward, outward, or laterally, depending on the species. The pistil consists of a pear-shaped ovary topped by three stigma prongs to receive pollen. Stigmas may be stubby or elongate, erect, flared, or recurved. The ovary may be greenish, white, purple, or near-black, and vary from 1/4 to 3/4 inch tall. Some are two-toned, whitish with purple top and stigmas. They contain 3 chambers, with a double row of seeds in each. There may be less than 100, or more than 200 ovules per ovary, but from 0 to 120 mature into seeds following pollenation. The ovary matures into a fleshy fruit that usually ruptures basally when ripe. Ants are usually on hand to aid the process, and carry off the seeds. So if you wish to collect seeds, you will have to anticipate the ripening, and collect the berries as they begin to soften. Most are purple or greenish, but *T. undulatum* has shiny scarlet berries.

All Trilliums are hardy perennials from fleshy rhizomes, rich in stored starch. This is a vital feature that permits the plant to maintain its vigor through a long warm, and then cold, dormant period from August to March or April, in most habitats. This structure is so efficient that even if the emerging shoot is browsed, or broken off before expanding in Spring, it has adequate reserves to carry it to the next year. This is a vital feature utilized in vegetative propagation. This also helps explain why seedlings require several years to build adequate reserves to produce a flower and fruit.

Trillium rhizomes are marked throughout by a series of rings. It is generally assumed that these are annual growth-rings, indicating age. With qualifications, this is true. They are scars from sheaths produced by the terminal bud around each young flower-shoot bud, and they serve to protect the developing shoot until it extends above ground. Usually two are produced for each shoot. In *T. rivale*, the rhizomes are marked also by prominent, oval shoot scars, complete with vascullar-bundle scars, but in many species these are difficult to discern. In the former, a count of shoot-scars on an unbranched rhizome will determine the age, but if counting sheath scars we must divide by two, or if a robust rhizome has been producing two flower shoots per year, we must divide by 4. This is explained in the accompanying diagram.

18

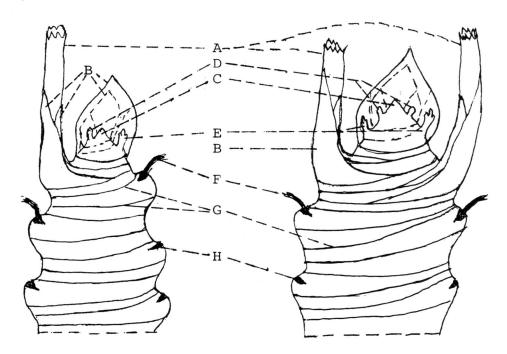

Left: A usual sculptured rhizome of a species like *Trillium sulcatum*, producing a single flowering shoot each year. This portion shows 6 seasons of growth with 12 sheath scars.

Right: A similar individual producing two flower shoots each year, with 3 seasons of growth, that has produced 12 sheath scars.

A. Flowering shoots of the present season
B. Basal sheaths
C. Growing point of rhizome
D. Youngest shoot primordia
E. Next season's young shoots
F. Remains of last season shoots
G. Sheath scars
H. Old shoot scars

Note: To improve understanding of this diagram, separation of paired shoots has been increased, and sheaths have been decreased in length and expanse.

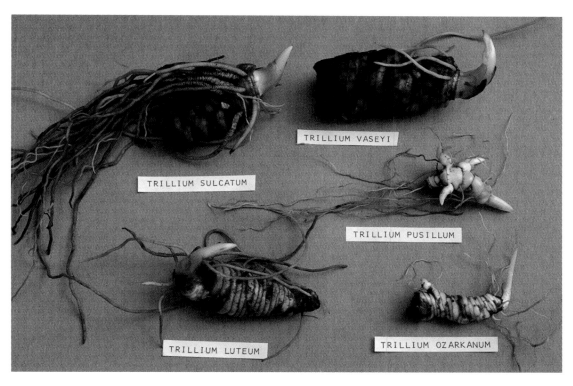

Comparison of *Trillium rhizome* types.

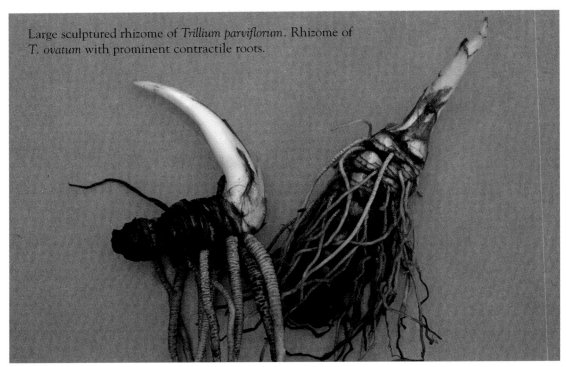

Large sculptured rhizome of *Trillium parviflorum*. Rhizome of *T. ovatum* with prominent contractile roots.

20

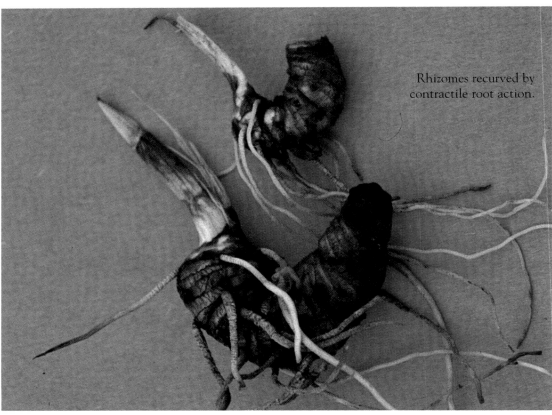

Rhizomes recurved by contractile root action.

Range Of Rhizome Characteristics

The differences between the rhizomes of various Trillium species is so great that some species can be identified by rhizomes alone. Furthermore, at least in the *T. pusillum - ozarkanum* complex, where the numerous entities are very similar above ground, the rhizomes reveal some clear-cut separations. A similar situation exists in the related genus Paris (in the broad-sense taxonomically).

Trillium rhizomes are either semi-erect or horzontally creeping. Each succeeding flowering shoot arises from a lateral bud beside the terminal bud, all within the protective sheaths terminating each rhizome or branch thereof. New roots arise quite exclusively from developing tips, not from old, mature rhizome segments. A few horizontally spreading species may produce slender, branching roots, but most produce, at least some, thick, somewhat corrugated roots, that are unbranched above. These are "contractile" roots that are able to shrink and contract, pulling the rhizome (at least the tip) downward. Except for this phenomenon, stout, erect rhizomes would emerge from the ground, despite their slow enlargement, and be fully exposed to weather, browsing, and physical damage. In some instances, rhizomes are curled into horse-she-like shapes as their tips are repeatedly pulled down and the reverse end curls upward. The extremely stout Paris japonica rhizomes maintain their horizontal position with strong contractile roots. Depending on species and habitat, roots disintegrate after 2 to 5 years.

The rhizomes of *T. rivale* are among the most distinctive. They are whitish, branching, lumpy, with conspicuous oval shoot scars revealing distinct bundle scars. They may also possess little clusters of bulbil propagules. The lumpiness may be exaggerated by their habit of squeezing between rocks in their usual wet talus slope habitat.

The unusually long, uniform, near cylindric, horizontal rhizomes of *T. recurvatum* are also clearly distinguishable from any other. Their dark shoot scars are prominent against well-developed white internodes. Thick contractile roots persist only a couple of years, so that even 6-inch, 15-year rhizomes are usually naked, except near the tip. Somewhat similar *T. stamineum* rhizomes are also unsculptured and smooth, with prominent pale internodes, but stem-scars are compressed with the sheath-scars, and branch buds arise freely on mature segments. These rhizomes are also notably thicker, and do not attain the extreme length of *T. recurvatum*.

The rhizomes of *T. chloropetalum*, *T. vaseyi*, *T. sulcatum* and similar species are notably sculptured as a result of enlargement at the base of each shoot scar. The prominence of sculpturing, texture, and color varies from species to species, and can be quite diagnostic.

Rhizome comparisons are particularly revealing and surprising in the *T. pusillum* complex, with representative entities scattered from Texas, the Ozarks, Alabama, Georgia, the Carolinas, Virginia, and Kentucky. Six or more taxa can be sorted out, and at least five different names are currently applied. All have very similar flowers, differing primarily in average dimensions, and length of the peduncle. All have smallish flowers with ruffle-edge, white petals turning rose. The relatively giant form in the Ozarks of Arkansas and Missouri, as well as western Kentucky, has unbranched, cylindric rhizomes with congested nodes. The diminutive frm in the lowlands of Virginia is a colony-former with freely-branching white rhizomes consisting of internodes at least as long as broad. The other

21

entities show kinship with one or the other of these, but can be separated by other characters.

Rhizome studies are valuable not only in Trillium classification, but also in the field of propagation. Even behavior in tissue culture is related to basic growth patterns.

PLANT COLORATION

Plant coloration, as revealed to the human eye, is determined by selective absorption of light rays by pigments. Surfaces that reflect all visible sunlight give the eye the impression of whiteness. Surfaces that absorbe all rays leave a void of blackness. Whiteness results when none of the wavelengths of light that make up the rainbow spectrum is out of balance with any of the others. Remove or reduce any one wavelength-color and the eye reacts to the non-balanced compliment of that color. Absorb all yellow, and the eye perceives blue, absorbe blue and the eye perceives yellow, absorb red and the eye perceives green, and vice versa. Plants have a variety of light-absorbing pigments. The pigments may be concentrated in discreet plastids or diffused in droplets of cell-sap. Plastid pigments are primarily green chlorophylls, which absorb most red light and lesser amounts of some other wavelengths, but reflect most green falling on them. Other plastid pigments include the yellow to orange carotenoids, which may be intermixed with chlorophylls, or in separate plastids. They absorb primarily blue and violet rays, and reflect yellow and orange. Water soluble cell-sap pigments, anthocyanins, absob light mostly in the green-yellow-orange range, and therefore appear red, blue, or violet. Their precise chemistry, and therefore light-absorbing qualities, can vary slightly with cell-sap

chemistry fluctuations. These can result from differences in chemistry of soil water taken up by roots, rate of sugar production by photosynthesis, direct effect of sunlight on tissues and pigments, and aging of tissues. Consequently these colors may be quite stable, or mutable and transient. It is common for purple or red anthocyanin pigments to develop in tissues when surplus sugars from photosynthesis are trapped by damaged conducting tissue. This can account for a normal green-leaf Trillium suddenly turning all purple. Examining the stem below ground usually reveals severe wounding from a rodent or insect.

In dealing with genetic control of color in Trilliums, we are obliged to describe what we observe, recognizing that many mechanisms of inheritence remain mystries, particularly the wonderfully compex, but repetitive, multicolored leaf patterns in plants such as *T. decipiens*. Leaf patterns are typical in sessile Trilliums, but do not occur in pedunculate species, except in freak individuals with variegated sectors. The rich green leaves of most pedunculate Trilliums can be attributed to the dense chloroplasts reflecting green and yellow light through a rather thin waxy cuticle cover over the leaf epidermis. In some species, *T. nivale* for example, a thicker cuticle renders a blue green color to the leaves. As the leaves of sessile-flowered species unfold, they frequently reveal patches of dark (sometimes near-black) tissue, colored by anthocyanin pigments, scattered across light green blades. As they mature, plastid density increases, producing a darker green tone, and obscuring the dark patches. Sometimes the anthocyanins disappear, leaving a uniform green leaf, as in *T. sessile*, but in others a subdued pattern remains, as in *T. maculatum*. Young flowers of all eastern American sessile Trilliums contain chloroplasts with both green

23

Three-year-old *T. decipiens* seedlings from
a single plant showing usual variation
in leaf pattern.

and yellow pigments. As flowers open, sepals remain green and often develop some anthocyanin purple streaking. Petals discontinue chlorophyll production, and sunlight destroys the initial supply, leaving carotenoids that give the petals a yellow color. Sometimes a limited chlorophyll production continues, resulting in petals of various shades of yellow-green. In others, anthocyanins accumulate as the petals expand, rendering deep-purple petals, or various bicolors. In *T. viridescens*, *T. viride*, and some others, petals may be rich green with purple basis.

TRILLIUMS AS MONOCOTS

As flowering plants evolved, they early-on headed in two distinct directions, and never looked back. Their naked-seed (without an enclosing ovary), non-flowering ancestors also gave rise to modern pines, firs etc.. In these the seed contains an embryo surrounded by reserve food. As germination occurs, the embryo sends down a root, and pushes up a shoot with multiple (commonly 6 or 7) green, slender leaves, the cotyledons. These are promptly replaced, in function by the true leaves developing on the young shoot. In Dicotyledonous flowering plants, reserve food is usually stored directly in two cotyledons, as part of the embryo, developing from fusion of a pollen nucleus with the egg cell. These may function only long enough to achieve germination, and then shrivel, or they may enlarge, and become green, functional leaves supporting the young plant while true leaves are developing. In the Monocotyledonous flowering plants, embryos contain little reserve food, and the single cotyledon may or may not develop into a green leaf. Reserve food is stored in a new tissue, the endosperm, produced when a second pollen nucleus fuses with a pair of nuclei in the ovule to initiate the triploid storage tissue. The embryo's cotyledon functions as an absorber of food from the endosperm during germination. It is easy to understand why orchids are so difficult to propagate from seeds in soil culture, when we consider that the tiny seeds are often free of endosperm food, and consequently essentially without reserves.

As Monocots, the seeds of Trilliums have a rather characteristic structure, but they also possess, uniformly, a feature shared by seeds of some Dicot plants such as Cyclamens, Bloodroots, Asarums, as well as some other Monocots. They not only have nutritive tissue within, but also possess a succulent, protein, external collar. This aril is of no nutritive value to the embryo, but it is very attractive to ants. They take the seeds in their dens, to feed on the aril, and then discard them - an efficient dissemination device, and an example of coevolutionary interdependence.

Trillium germination is at first concealed below ground. The embryo consists of two divergent primordia and a single cotyledon, which at first functions as an absorber of food stored in the endosperm. The cotyledon elongates, pushing a tiny tuber outward from the seed coat while the basal primordium is producing the first root. The arched cotyledon continues to enlarge, emerging from the ground, turning erect, changing from yellow to bright green, and functiong as the first photosynthetic leaf. By the time the cotyledonary leaf shrivels, the apical bud has produced a protective sheath around itself, and

a lateral bud that will expand the following Spring into a somewhat larger simple leaf. Usually two lopsided-cylinder sheaths (one inside the other) are produced each year thereafter. The tuber and simple leaf increase in size each year. In small species, such as *T. pusillum*, a three-leaved plant may be produced by the third or fourth cycle, and flowering will occur the next year. *T. rivale* may require five years to produce a 3-leaf plant, but it usually flowers the same year. In more robust species, with large rhizomes, such as *T. erectum* and *T. kurabayashii*, a 3-leaved plant may be produced 2 or 3 years before acquiring enough reserves to produce a flower. Variations in Trillium seed behavior will be dealt with under "Trillium Propagation".

Characteristically, the leaves of Monocots produce vascular tissue in veins of uniform size, parallel to each other, extending from the leaf-base to the tip. This is readily observed in leaves of corn, iris, lily-of-the-valley, and palm leaves. Although Trilliums are Monocots,

Germinating seeds.

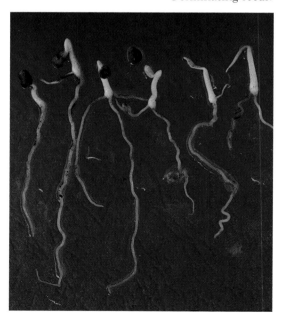

they depart from most of their kin by possessing branching net venation. They usually have three main veins in each leaf. These give rise to branches which extend into smaller and smaller divisions, until the fine capillaries connect in a net pattern. This is precisely the system found in leaves of Dicots such as roses, oaks, and beans. A Eur- Asian group of species in the related genus Paris, also Monocots, shares this uniqueness with Trilliums.

ORIGINALITY AMONG TRILLIUMS

Once we have become acquainted with the usual structure and behavior of Trilliums, we are repeatedly confronted by the unusual. It is these mavericks that keep gardeners ever young. In at least one instance, the maverick has given rise to a distinct species population. *Trillium apetalon* of Japan and Sakhalin produces no petals at all, and its sepals are like purple petals. It sometimes hybridizes with other Asian species giving rise to hybrids that may,or may not, have petals. In the case of *T. smallii* in northern Japan we have a hybrid species that may have 3 normal petals, and six stamens, or no petals and 9 stamens. In other aberrant individual Trilliums, all stamens may develop into petals, producing a "double" flower with 9 petals. In extreme cases, a Trillium may produce 30 or more petals, plus 3 normal sepals, but no stamens or pistils. Unsymmetrical flowers with only one or two petals, and odd numbers of stamens, also occur. Not only do the numbers of petals vary, but also the size and shape of petals in a given species, may vary greatly. A good example is *T. flexipes* in which the white petals may barely exceed 1/2 inch or be nearly 2 1/2 inches in length, and from 1/4 inch to over 1 inch in width. Furthermore, this ancient species with a wide range, may hold its flowers

very erect, or horizontal, or somewhat declined beneath its leaves. Only 4 species have consistently nodding flowers, usually below the leaves. Of course, no sessile species have nodding flowers.

A fascinating characteristic that evolved early among sessile populations, but not in pedunculate populations, is the presence of mottled or patterned leaves. This is achieved by the irregular scattering of patches of leaf tissues with very different pigment composition. Anthocyanin pigments in cell vocuoles (internal droplets) can produce purple coloring of various tones. When combined with the normal green plastid pigments, a pattern of dark blotches results. This is usually most dramatic in young leaves, before the full complement of chlorophyll has formed, and more effectively masked the anthocyanins. The leaf patterning is obviously under intricate genetic control. In some species the mottling is rather ephemeral, hit and miss splotches, undetectable by the time fruits are ripening. In other species, a quite fixed pattern, of multiple color areas, persists to maturity. The pattern in a single leaf may consist of distinct areas of dark purple, purple-green, silver, silver-green, and dark green. These patterns are characteristic of virtually all of the nine or ten presumably youthful species of the Southern Piedmont and Coastal Plain. It has attained a Zenith of artistry in *T. decipiens* and *T. underwoodii*. In the garden, the foliage of these plants outshines the flowers of most.

Why is it that this characteristic is not met with in pedunculate species? Even the white-flowered species can produce anthocyanin pigments. I have observed occasional purple-leaved *T. ovatum*, *T. erectum*, and *T. grandiflorum*, and if the stem of a green-leaved plant is injured, so as to interfere with translocation of food manufactured in the leaves, the plant produces anthocyanins, and

25

T. decipiens with 4 sepals and
an anther on 1 petal

Trillium undulatum with 6 leaves, 5 sepals,
4 petals, and 8 stamens.

26

Multistem *T. cuneatum.*
Shoots with 6 to 9 leaves,
but no flowers.

Two *T. sessile* with 6 leaves plus
flowers, and a *T. cuneatum* plant
with 6 leaves, but no flowers.

leaves turn purple. The important difference is that there is no genetic control to produce a pattern.

Another anomaly occasionally encountered is the replacement of flowers with extra whorls of leaves. Two or three whorls may develop, close-set, one above the other, in staggered arrangement, producing a stem terminated by a green "flower" of 6 or nine leaves. The leaves of each higher whorl are somewhat smaller than the preceding ones, and no true flower parts appear. Occasionally six-leaved plants are topped by normal flowers.

GENETIC CHARACTER OF TRILLIUMS

So far we have concentrated on the visible characteristics of Trilliums. Obviously all of these traits are controlled by living genetic material in the cells, primarily in the chromosomes in cell nuclei. Trillium cells and chromosomes are relatively large, compared to those of many organisms. The number of kinds of chromosomes in Trilliums is conversely quite small. We are indebted largely to researchers from Japan, especially H. Matsuma, I. Fukuda, T. Haga and Masataka Kurabayashi for much of our understanding of Trillium taxonomic relationships as revealed by chromosomal studies. Throughout the genus, the genes are grouped into basically five kinds of chromosomes, so the normal cells of Trillium plants, which have two of each kind, have 10 chromosomes. This applies to all North American species, but only the primitive T. kamtschaticum in Asia. Three of the Asian species are stable, fertile populations with 20 chromosome or 4 times the prime number. These include T. apetalon, T. tschonoskii, and T. govanianum. The only two other Asian species, plus several sterile hybrids, are derived forms arising from natural crosses between T. apetalon, T. kamtschaticum, and T. tschonoskii.

It is truly remarkable that sexual reproduction in flowering plants, with all the intricacies, proceeds as flawlessly as it does. The flawlessness, however, is not absolute. During formation of pollen and egg cells, the chromosome complement of body cells is reduced to half, or 5 chromosomes in Trilliums. During fertilization the typical body cell number of 10 is regained. But if the pollen from a 10 chromosome plant fertilizes the egg of a 20 chromosome plant we have a serious problem. The resulting embryo, with 15 chromosomes in each cell, can grow into a quite typical Trillium, but in producing pollen and egg cells it is confused. Its imperfect seeds are aborted, leaving the plant sterile. But if the plant manages to produce pollen and egg cells with the unreduced number of 15 chromosomes in each, the pairing of chromosomes during cell division meets no problems, and a new individual develops with 30 chromosomes in each cell. From then on, the plant has few problems, reproducing itself with 15 chromosome pollen and egg cells, and 30 chromosome plants. Since they have 6 times the basic 5 chromosomes, they are called hexaploids. Such a process apparently resulted in the development of T. smallii and T. hagae with 30 chromosomes in each. Interestingly, the sterile hybrid form of T. X hagae with 15 chromosomes is sometimes encountered where the parents, T. kamtschaticum (10) and T. tschonoskii (20) occur together.

From this discussion it is obvious that, while chromosome numbers exhibit limited variation in Trilliums, especially American species, the gene complements on the chromosomes must differ appreciably. If this were not the case, we would expect little occurrence of hybrid sterility. Until now,

I know of few efforts at hybridizing sessile with pedunculate species, and I have not observed such hybrids in the wild, despite identical chromosome numbers.

Self-sterility within species of Trillium does not appear to be a common factor. I have encountered little difficulty in successful self-pollination of individuals. This is a boon to plant breeders, as it enables the establishment of superior, true-breeding strains.

As to chromosomal anomalies, many types probably occur in nature. Some would have little chance of being perpetuated without assistance from humans. Occasional specimens with 15 chromosomes have been reported in at least two American species (*T. flexipes* and *T. erectum*). Also, fragments of chromosomes may be present or absent, and the range of variations is endless. For these reasons, we are obliged to paint our concept of each species with a sufficiently broad brush to present a realistically inclusive picture of its natural populations.

Years of intensive field and garden studies reveal a very complex, but fascinating, array of plants that are not always divisible into clearly defined species. It is easily understandable that keen observers of Trilliums proceed from an early recognition of distinct types to an ever-darkening cloud of utter-confusion. Any guru who has a ready answer to all questions of Trillium taxonomy convincingly portrays either lack of experience, or self-deception. Still, for purpose of communications, we are obligated to define and name the types we recognize and cultivate. To this end, meaningful conclusions require a consideration of time, space and geologic history. Certain characteristics common throughout the genus are discernible, and these play important roles in conclusions reached here. It is the distinct and consistent departures from the base characters that allow us to recognize and name separate species. When a considerable variety of plants is observed in a single population we interpret this as a modern, genetically complex, single species populations, that may, or many not, have received genetic material from another species in the past. Variation in a population is common in most plants, and by itself, does not suggest hybridization.

CHAPTER 5

A Bit of History
Magnolias, Trilliums and Paris

Magnolia-type trees apparently evolved during the mid Cretaceous Period, some 100 million years ago, but our modern forms probably all arose since the the end of the Cretaceous, about 65 million years ago, when many kinds of animals, and plants became extinct. For the ensuing 40 million years or more, the Earth was mostly bathed in warm, dry or humid, tropical climates. In the land-mass that was to become North America, tropical forests extended above 50 N. latitude (southern Canada), and broad-leaved evergreens and palms grew as far north as Hudson Bay. Since Trilliums have undoubtedly been associated with deciduous forests throughout their existence, an understanding of the evolution of this vegetation-type should be enlighening. Deciduous Magnolias have been a component of deciduous forests throughout this time.

In the early cretaceous the map of Earth was vastly different than at present. Land formations were lower, seas were higher, Africa and South America had not yet separated from the southern continent of Gondwana, and Laurasia represented a northern mass that was to give rise to North America and Asia. What is now Europe was little more than islands in a shallow sea. Much of what is now western North America and Central America was then under shallow seas. The mild, humid climate supported tropical forests of tree ferns, seed-ferns, giant horsetails, and broad-leaved evergreens, virtually all now

extinct. It was during these conditions, over 100 million years ago, that flowering plants began to evolve. Since the history must be reconstructed from pollen analyses, fragments of twigs, leaves, fruits, and seeds, the details of the early history must remain obscure, but evolutionary stages in vegetation types, and constituent plant families can be ascertained.

Magnolia-like trees are among the first flowering plants to appear in the fossil record. They were broad-leaved evergreens competing with trees that had probably dominated the tropical forests for more than 100 million years. The immeidate ancestors of the first flowering plants, is a puzzle we may never solve, though theories abound. By 65 million ago, numerous families of flowering plants had evolved, but they apparently seldom established dominant communities. Soon thereafter the scene changed dramatically. Not only dinosaurs, but also much of the dominant plant life was gone, and soon replaced by rapidly diversifying mammals, birds, and insects, together with diversifying plant communities dominated by flowering plants closely linked to the animals serving as pollinators and seed dispersers. Conifer Forests persisted, but in mild temperate climates, shade-tolerant, fast-growing deciduous forests took over, relegating the conifers to colder, dryer, higher altitudes, higher latitudes, or coastal fog belts. As flowering plants diversified, they eventually occupied nearly all availaable habitats. Grasses appeared about 60

29

million years ago. By mid Miocene, some 15 million years ago, grasslands occupied vast areas where horses, camels, and antelope grazed. By Pliocene time, about 5 million years ago, a group of compact, ground-hugging, flowering plants, of extreme hardiness developed into the circumpolar Tundra north of the forests and onto the mountains above tree-line.

By the end of the Cretaceous, the rift between Africa and South America was complete and the separation continues to expand to this day. In the meantime, seas gradually receded, and western mountains arose, connecting North, South, and Central America. From about 100 million to 20 million years ago, North America and Asia were connected by Beringia a broad land bridge across the north Pacific. For perhaps 150 million years neither East Asia nor Southeastern North America have experienced radical geographic or climatic disruptions, except for the Cretaceous-ending catastrophe. This helps in understanding the remarkable similarity between present day floras in East Asia, and Southeast North America, a flora that, in not too distant times, was uninterrupted from Eastern North America, northward and westward across Canada, Alaska, and Beringia to Asia. Isolation of these areas for the past twenty million years or so has allowed for independent evolution, but many species have scarcely-distingiushable representatives in each region.

The first lily-type flowers appeared during the Eocene Epoch, some 40 million years ago. They were probably tropical, evergreen, perennials. They rapidly diversified into many growth-forms: tree-like, vining sorts, bulbous, and rhizomatous. Early on, several became intimately associated with temperate deciduous forest communites. These developed an ephemeral habit, activating in early Spring, before tree leaves expanded, flowering, fruiting, and retiring to underground storage organs until next Spring. Among these were the progenitors of Trilliums. Unfortunately, they left no similar descendents, or fossils recognizable as pre-trillium ancestors. We can only speculate on this matter. Only one group of living plants exhibits enough similarity to Trilliums to suggest a near common ancestor. They make up the roughly 20 members of the Paris complex, which, like Trilliums are associated with deciduous forest. While Paris (Wheel Lilies) and Trilliums share many characters, they could hardly be derived one from the other directly. Paris species occur from Japan and Eastern Asia to Western Europe. Trilliums are essentially southeastern North American plants with a few species in the West from California to British columbia, and a lesser number of closely-knit kinds in Japan and China. As in Eastern North America, Trilliums in East Asia are usualy found in decidous forest. Even in our Pacific Northwest, where conifers predominate, Trilliums are commonly associated with decidous trees and shrubs, oaks, maples, dogwood, snowberry, etc., or seek out exposed marginal sites.

The progenitors of Trilliums and Paris probably evolved in temperate climates from more tropical ancestors. They probably had broad, entire, net-veined leaves in variable numbers on leafy stems. They had multi-chambered compound pistils. They had poorly-differentiated, green perianth parts, variable in number, and comparable numbers of slender stamens with large sticky pollen. Early on, basal leaves were reduced to non-photosynthetic sheaths protecting the shoot tips, and the stem leaves were restricted to a single whorl. In the different species of Paris, the number ranges from 4 to 10 leaves, in Trillium it is invariably three. In Paris the petals are inconspicuous, slender, yellow to purple filaments (or absent) and the sepals are prominent (green, purplish or white). Some early progenitors may have had a continuous distribution between Asia and North America, but evolution proceeded in diffferent directions in the two areas. With subsequent loss, by extinction, of the ancient forms we can only speculate. An interesting pattern of diversification has evolved in Paris. Some species have very inconspicuous green flowers, and rapidly spreading slender rhizomes able to colonize an area in a hurry. At present only five species are recognized in this group but collectively they span the breadth of the range of distribution of the Paris complex from England to Japan.

The most unique member of the complex is found only in the mountains of Honshu Japan. It is an impressive plant, to 30" tall from a stout rhizome, with 8-10 leaves up to

Paris polyphylla with 7 leaves, 5 broad green sepals and 5 slender yellow petals.

12x3", 8-10 snowy white sepals to 2x1", and 0-10 slendeer white petals. This species is an allo-octaploid with 40 chromosomes, and no living near kin. Fukuda and Takamatsu suggested in 1969 that *Paris japonica* is a natural hybrid between *Paris verticillata* and *Trillium tschonoskii*. It is often referred to a seperate genus as *Kinugasa japonica*. A hybrid

Paris japonica rhizome

origin from these two parents is rather incomprehensible. *Trillium tschonoskii* has 20 chromosomes, a stout rhizome, showy white petals attractive to certain insects, and seeds with a fleshy coat. *Paris verticillata* has 10 chromosomes, slendeer, running rhizomes, green sepals, inconspicuous, yellowish-filament petals, probably attracting different insects, and seeds with non-fleshy coats. These two species flower more than a month apart. While *Paris japonica* is certainly the showiest species, it is by no means the largest.

About 16 species of this complex have been assigned to a group presently listed in the genus *Daiswa*. Some interesting and attractive plants are included. All occur in Southeast Asia. All have stout rhizomes, long or short. They have fleshy fruits and fleshy scarlet seed coats. The pistil is angular with 3-10 stout styles, and often a stigmatic disc. The largest species is certainly *Daiswa (Paris) hainanensis* from South China. It grows to six feet tall with a five foot flower stalk. It usually has six leaves up to 12-6". The most wide-spread species is *Daiswa (Paris) polyphylla*. It occcures from Himalayas to China, Burma, Taiwan, and Thailand. Consequently it is unusually variable. It is 1-3 feet tall with 6-12 leaves, which may have purple petioles, or may be sessile. The 4-7 sepals are usually green with some purple at the base. The equal number of slender petals are usually yellowish. Some dwarf forms have been collected in the mountains of Sechuan, China. If these can be propagated and distributed, they should be choice garden plants. they are only about 6 inches tall, and some have large, bright yelow sepals and petals. They have been described as *Daiswa polyphylla* var *nana* and var. *alba*.

Actually, there are many members of the Paris complex that could be fascinating garden plants, but most have been unattainable.

Among these is *Daiswa violacea*, a small species about eight inches tall with variegated leaves and sepals. The variegation is in the form of whitish veining as in *Arum italicum*. Its leaves are usually purple on the underside.

While members of the Paris Complex usually have 10 or 20 chromosomes, like Trilliums, the likelyhood of hybridization between the two groups, even in the garden, is remote for several reasons. Trilliums are mostly early risers, flowering weeks or months before Paris species. Most members of both groups are self-fertile, and self-pollination is common in seed production. Vast differences in flowers between the two groups accounts for different insects visting them. Only a few Asiatic Trilliums grow in association with Paris species. Unlike Trilliums, a few species of Paris can achieve dispersal quite effectively by strictly vegetative means.

There is one outstanding exception to the above summary. In scattered colonies between 9,000 and 12,000 feet elevation in the Himalayas from Kashmir to Bhutan is a maverick that may well illustrate parallel evolution. *Trillium govanianum* has an elongate but stout, rhizome like many Trilliums and Daiswa members of Paris. Its leaves and all flower parts are in whorls of 3 as in all Trilliums, bu the leaves have prominent petioles, elongate tips, and texture resembling some Paris species. Furthermore sepals and petals are small, very slender, and purple to greenish. Stamens are much smaller than in any other Trillium, and the small globose ovary contains non-fleshy seeds. It has 20 chromosomes like many Paris, but unlike American Trilliums which have 10. This species is commonly referred to as *Trillidium govanianum*, and may have had a common ancestor with Paris species.

CHAPTER 6

TRILLIUM AND MAGNOLIA ASSOCIATION

Being among the oldest families of flowering plants, Magnolias have had ample opportunity to invade all exposed land contiguous with site of origin. Fossil records indicate their former presence over most of what has become North America, at least to Hudson Bay, and west across Alaska and Beringia through most of Asia into Europe. As various Trilliums and Paris evolved, they most likely found themselves in the company of Magnolias in mixed-deciduous forests. The earliest kinds of Magnolias were most likely tropical broad-leaved evergreens. For the past 50 million years, cooling, drying climates have favored the developing deciduous forests over much of this area, and in turn, relegating broad-leaved evergreens southward toward the Equator. This, together with Pleistocene glaciation, has greatly restricted Magnolia distribution in Asia as well as North America. Magnolias no longer occur west of the Himalayas. They are absent from Europe and Western Asia. Likewise, they no longer exist in the wild west of eastern Texas, so Trilliums of our Pacific-Northwest woodlands have lost their Magnolia-connection.

Neither Trilliums nor Magnolias ever reached the Southern Hemisphere. Interestingly, even modern Magnolia species have retained their primitive dependence on pollination by beetles. Like Trilliums, Magnolias are subordinate members in deciduous forests, dependent on the association, but never dominating. They do not choose exposed sites, or grow in pure stands. One Magnolia-Family member is, however, a prominant (sometimes dominant) member of many deciduous forests east of the Mississippi River from North Florida to the Great Lakes and Massachusetts. It is the Tulip Poplar (*Liriodendron tulipifera*). Its only surviving close relative, *Liriodendron chinense*, is found in central China in the company of *Trillium tschonoskii*, *Magnolia sprengeri*, and *Magnolia officinalis*. The extensive range of the American Tulip Poplar overlaps the ranges of almost all Eastern American Trillium species.

In Japan there are only a few species of Trilliums, but the wide-spread and prominent deciduous forest tree, *Magnolia kobus*, is often associated with *Trillium apetalon* in mixed forests. Other species of Magnolias and Trilliums sometimes keep them company.

In eastern North America the sorting out of Trilliums and Magnolias is quite independent, yet interesting associations have resulted. By far, the best known American species is *Magnolia grandiflora*, our only completely evergreen species. It is grown as an ornamental in almost all warm-temperate areas of our Globe. It borders the wetlands in our Coastal Plains, and its shallow, all-consuming, root-system, together with its black-out dense canopy, eliminate all competition beneath it. Don't look for Trilliums there. All other species are essentially deciduous. Only M. *virginiana* is semi-evergreen, but its rather open canopy is little deterrent to Spring herbs beneath it. This is also a Coastal Plain tree, but it enters the Piedmont along streams. From the Carolinas to Georgia and Alabama, *Trillium maculatum*, *T. cuneatum*, and *T. catesbaei* may share its habitat. In Louisiana and East Texas, *Trilliium ludovicianum* and *T. gracile* sometimes occur with it.

Perhaps the most impressive deciduous tree in Eastern North America is *Magnolia macrophylla*. With leaves near 3 feet long, and a foot wide, and fragrant white flowers over one foot broad, it commands attention. In the Northern part of its range in Kentucky it associates with *Trillium grandiflorum* and *T. erectum*. In the Piedmont of Georgia it is accompanied by *Trillum cuneatum*, *T. rugelii* and *T. catesbaei*. In the Coastal Plain it is joined by *Trillium maculatum*, *T. reliquum*, and *T. underwoodii*, with *Trillium stamineum* appearing in west Alabama and Mississippi.

Magnolia tripetala is nearly as impressive as the last species, but there are distinct differences. The broad leaves may approach two feet in length, but they have wedge-shaped bases, whereas M. *macrophylla* has prominent ears. Its creamy flowers are large but only half the size of M. *macrophylla's*, and they emit the odor of a Stink-horn fungus. This tree is not a good choice for home entrance planting, but it is a majestic addition to a woodland. Its northern range extends from Ohio into southern Pennsylvania, where it cohorts with *Trilliums grandiflorum*, *T. erectum*, *T. sessile*, *T. flexipes*, *T. cernuum*, and occasionally *T. nivale*. From north Georgia into Tennessee and North Carolina *Magnolia tripetala* occurs in widely-scattered colonies with *Trillium cuneatum*, *T. catesbaei*, *T. vaseyi*, *T. rugelii*, and occasionally *T. decumbens*. In the

southern-most part of its range in Georgia and Alabama it is joined by *T. maculatum*.

The very hardy Cucumber Magnolia, M. *acuminata*, ranges as far north as southern Ontario. It is usually found with *Trillium erectum*, *T. grandiflorum*, *T. cernuum*, *T. flexipes*, or *T. sessile*. In the south, colonies of this Magnolia occur with brighter yellow flowers, and some with smaller stature, that have been named var. *cordata*. They occur from Tennessee to Georgia, Alabama, and Louisiana. *Trillium luteum*, *T. cuneatum*, *T. catesbaei*, or *T. vaseyi* may occur with these colonies.

In the mountains from West Virginia to north Georgia are colonies of *Magnolia fraseri* with large eared leaves, and large creamy, delightfully-fragrant flowers. This is the only Magnolia that associates with the Painted Trillium, *T. undulatum*, but *Trillium grandiflorum*, *T. erectum*, and *T. cuneatum* may also join some colonies.

Magnolia pyramidata is a small tree in the Coastal Plain from southwest Georgia across Alabama to southeast Texas. It resembles M. *fraseri* but with smaller eared leaves, and smaller fragrant flowers. *Trillium maculatum*, *T. ludoviciana* and several other species are sometimes associated with colonies of this Magnolia.

It would be fascinating, indeed, to have access to a video history of the vegetation of eastern North America for the last 65 million years. That would, of course, eliminate the mysteries that researchers delight in trying to solve, and might lead to boredom. But certain conclusions seem justified. Eastern American Magnolias represent a quite stable group of species, and have regained little of their preglacial territory, but Trilliums appear to be genetically restless. In the past three centuries much Trillium habitat has been lost to clearing for agriculture, and, recently, for urban development. As this process continues, it is likely that wide-spread species will have their ranges interrupted into isolated populations. The limited gene-pool, in each of these outlier populations, would stabilize some recessive characters formerly masked by dominants in the overall population. In time, they could be recognized as taxonomically distinct. This process very likely accounts for the diversity of recognizable sessile Trillium types in the Southeast today, and the process is on-going. Actually the restlessness is strictly limited. There appears to be no interchange between sessile and pedunculate Trilliums, nor between Trilliums and any other genera. There also are few lineal departures that could result in new genera.

CHAPTER 7

TRILLIUMS IN THE WILD

While it is not the intent of this work to produce a new taxonomic monograph of the genus Trillium, problems of classification will be dealt with. Since our emphasis is on Trilliums as garden plants, natural diversity is of greater interest than establishing an average for the characteristics of each species. Of course, if we are to communicate intelligently, we must take cognizance of the latter as well. Plant taxonomists may understandably envy animal taxonomists, whose subjects, are mostly unisexual, and have many more isolating mechanisms to keep species distinct than are possessed by plants. Since higher animals are mobile, have sight, and may be vocal, they are able to attract or select mates of their own choosing. This tends to enhance the establishment of pure- breeding populations recognized as species, and reduces the likelihood of hybridization. Matings among plants, rooted-in-place, are far more chancy, despite the fact that many plants, including Trilliums, have perfect-flowers, both male and female organs, and can undergo self-fertilization.

Considering these facts, it is actually remarkable that plants have evolved populations that are sufficiently similar among themselves, yet sufficiently distinct from others to be dealt with as species. Even so, there is a possibility of hybridization bringing an infusion of alien characteristics which may diffuse through the population indefinitely.

For these reasons, the concept of "species" in plant classification must remain nebulous. It is, after all, a man-made tool of great usefulness, but not writ-in-stone. Plants occur in nature as individual members of variable populations. Only when a clear discontinuity in variation exists between members of similar populations is the species concept fully realized. A less confining term, that greatly facilitates discussion, has therefore found its way into common usage. A "taxon" (plural=taxa) may refer to a clearly-defined species, or any poulation of the species with a more restricted definition. The most restrictive definition is reserved for taxa in which all individuals are uniformly alike, because they have been propagated vegetatively from a single original specimen, or from a highly controlled seed production process. These "cultivars" are sometimes referred to as clones, and may be produced by stem, leaf, or root-cuttings, or by micropropagation from pieces of dividing tissue. It is cultivar propagation that can bring to gardeners the most desirable Trilliums, and at the same time, stem the decimation of wild populations.

Consistency is a very desirable goal that can doubtfully be maintained without becoming absurd. Nevertheless, in the discussion to follow, we intend to standardize certain terms and common names. One of the most serious problems in horticultural communications is careless use of language. If we say what we mean, we should be able to communicate effectively, so long as we are using the same language, and same dictionary. Unnecessary technical terms will be avoided, but certain terms have no common equivalents, and should be a part of every serious gardeners vocabulary. Most of these terms are in any Webster Dictionary. Even the latinized names of plants cease to be mysteries when we apply logic and the dictionary to them. After all, many words in everyday usage came from the same Greek and Latin words that gave us the descriptive names of plants:

grandiflorum - large or grand flower
pauciflorum - few flowers - paucity
albidum, album - albino - white
rubrum - ruby - red
roseum - rose
umbellatum - umbrella-like

But we can have a problem if we try to deal with a plant name in separate parts. You may have encountered the statement that *Trillium* is the genus name, and luteum is a species name. In truth, luteum is very little by itself. It is an adjective requiring a noun to give it identity. And when Trilliums are concerned, it must be used very carefully. There are at least 23 species of sessile-flowered Trilliums in North America, and while only one is properly called *Trillium luteum*, most of the others have luteum forms with yellow flowers, while the majority have purple flowers. Since most sessile Trilliums now recognized as distinct species were at some time identified as *T. sessile*, or a variety of that species, there is still considerable confusion. A recent publication presents a photo of true *T. luteum* labeled *T. sessile* var. *luteum*, a very different taxon.

In the present work all Trilliums with flowers raised above the leaves on a stalk (peduncle) are given common names as "Wake-Robins", and all sessile-flowered species are called "Toad-Shades". This represents a standardization of a partial similar use of these common names. No hybridization is known between members of these two groups.

Trilliums, in all their diversity, are yet to be discovered as garden plants. This is due, in part, to our inability to come to terms with the conservation issue. We are told by some conservation spokespersons, as well as some nurseries, that all Trilliums offered for sale are wild collected, and therefore, purchase of these plants decimates our woodlands. Historically there is substantial truth in this conclusion, but it does not deal realistically with the problems. Many Trilliums are excellent garden plants. Do we choose to grow them, or covet them under a shroud of guilt, or do we offer information on propagation, and cultivation, so as to assure a supply of superior plants, a high rate of survival, and greater satisfaction to all? A very depressing problem arose with mass-marketing ventures, in which thousands of Trilliums and other wild plants were taken from the wild, bulk shipped, stuffed into plastic bags with a picture header, and hung on store racks for sale. These plants do not tolerate handling like tulips and daffodils. In some cases, survival for more than a year was less than 2%.

Actually, propagating and marketing Trilliums is not difficult if there simple requirments are met. Richard Fraser of Thimble Farm in British Columbia is among those who have launched such programs. Furthermore, landowners with substantial native Trillium populations should be encouraged to farm them, rather than selling the land for development. Natural propagation in such colonies can be enhanced several fold with proper care. We have often been invited to participate in Trillium rescues, when highways or development threatened substantial populations. To be sure, our woodlands are diminishing.

CHAPTER 8

A KEY TO THE SPECIES OF TRILLIUMS

Keys are useful tools, but with distinct limitations. They are intended as aids in determining identity of unrecognized plant specimens, but they serve other functions as well. A key is a catalog of all species described in a taxonomic group, and therefore lists the options available. It attempts to zero in on the most consistent, visible differences between species, so can not easily utilize phenology, chromosomal properties, or other subtle differences. Keys facilitate a preliminary identification, which should then be confirmed by studying a detailed description, and illustration, if available.

For various reasons, individual specimens are not always keyable to a species name.

Some specimens are natural hybrids, and a key may indicate possible parents. Keys utilize average or most usualy traits. Unique specimens will, obviously, not fit all of these featuers. Under cultivation, some of these may be enhanced or altered.

Keys are intended to reveal the persistent genetic distinctness of species, but the expression of inherited traits is always tempered by environmental influences, such as light intensity, temperature, soil chemistry, rainfall, humidity, etc. These factors can affect size of plant parts, pigmentation, and texture, as well as natural propagation.

I. ASIATIC SPECIES - all with stalked flowers, leaves uniformly green

	subgenus *Trillium*
1. Leaves with prominent petioles. Himalayan	*Trillium govanianum*
1. Leaves sessile.	2.
2. Flowers white.	3.
3. Sepal tips drawn-out (acuminate). Himalayas to Japan	*T. tschonoskii*
3. Sepal tips wedge-shaped, not acuminate.	4.
4. Stamens longer than pistil. China-Siberia-Japan.	*T. kamtschaticum*
4. Stamens shorter than pistil. North Japan.	5.
5. Capsule small, conical.	(Triploid) *T. x hagae*
5. Capsule plump ovoid.	(Hexaploid) *T. hagae*
2. Flowers red-purple. Northern Japan.	6.
6. No petals, sepals purple.	*T. apetalon*
6. Some petals usually present.	7.
7. Capsule large, to 25 mm (1"), petals 3-0, fertile.	*T. smallii*
7. Capsule small, to 13 mm (1/2") petals 3-0, sterile hybrids.	8.

38

8. Sepals broad-ovate , Length : Width = 3 : 2   *T. x yezoense*
8. Sepals narrow-ovate, L : W = 2 : 1   *T. x miyabeanum*

II. North American species :

A. Flowers sessile, leaves usually mottled. = "Toadshades"   subgenus Phyllantherum
  1. Leaves with petioles.   2.
    2. Petioles usually more than 5 cm (2"+) long, leaves uniform green, purple flowers
      near soil surface. Northwest.   *T. petiolatum*
    2. Petioles less than 2.5 cm (1"), leaves mottled, stems tall, sepals recurved,
      petals purple or yellow. East.   *T. recurvatum*
  1. Leaves sessile.   3.
    3. Western species, usually weakly mottled.   4.
      4. Flowers white.   5.
        5. Pistil & stamens purple, also purple petal forms.   *T. chloropetalum* var. *giganteum*
        5.Pistil & stamens white or greenish.   6.
          6. Petals narrow, L : W = 5:1   *T. parviflorum*
          6. Petals larger, broader, L : W = 3:1   *T. albidum*
      4. Flowers purple or yellowish.   7.
        7. Petals purple, very slender L : W = 9:1   *T. angustipetalum*
        7. Petals larger, broader.   8.
          8. Petals purple, broad, 3-4" long, stamen : pistil length = 5 : 4,
            leaves coarse-veiny, distinctly mottled.   *T. kurabayashii*
          8. Petals greenish-yellow to purple, ca. 3" long, stamen : pistil length = 2 : 1,
            leaves smooth-succulent, obscure-mottled.   *T. chloropetalum*
    3. Eastern species, usually prominently mottled. Flowers purple to yellow, not white.   9.
        9. Stems decumbent, leaves resting on litter.   10.
          10. Upper stem velvety and thickened.   *T. decumbens*
          10. Stem smooth (glabrous) and of uniform thickness.   *T. reliquum*
        9. Stems erect.   11.
          11. Leaf mottling obscure, disappears early. Flowers purple,
            rarely yellow.   *T. sessile*
          11. Leaves marbled 2-3 colors or more.   12.
            12. Flowers always yellow, leaves light green.   13.
              13. Bright yellow, lemon scent, leaves may lose marbling.   *T. luteum*
              13. Pale yellow, clove scent, leaves retain tricolor marbling.   *T. discolor*
            12.Flowers purple, purple/green, or yellow. Leaves darker multicolor.   14.
              14. Petals horizontal, twisted propeller-like.   *T. stamineum*
               14. Petals erect.   15.
                15. Anthers open inwardly.   16.
                  16. Ovary 3-angled, very early flowering.   *T. maculatum*
                  16. Ovary 6-angled, midseason.   17.

17. Rhizome slender horizontal-branching.   *T. lancifolium*

17. Rhizome stout, not free-branching.   18.

   18. Pistil ca. 1/2 length of stamens.   *T. gracile*

   18. Pistil ca. 3/4 length of stamens.   19.

    19. Ovary sharply constricted above.   *T. foetidissimum*

    19. Ovary not sharply constricted.   *T. cuneatum*

15. Anthers open laterally.   20.

    20. Leaves obscurely mottled, petals greenish with purple base.   21.

     21. Leaves dusted with white specks (stomates) on top. Stamens 1.5 x pistil height.   *T. viride*

     21. Leaves not obviously dusted. Stamens 2+ x pistil height.   *T. viridescens*

    20. Leaves prominently multicolored with silvery central zone.   22.

    22. Petals narrow, to 2" long, usually greenish above purple base.   *T. ludovicianum*

    22. Petals to 3"+ long, broad, usually purple.   23.

     23. Stems 2 1/2 + x leaf length, sepals divergent, L : W = 3:1   *T. decipiens*

     23. Stems 1 1/2 x leaf length, sepals near horizontal, 4:1 L:W.   *T. underwoodii*

A. Flowers stalked, leaves uniformly green. Wake-Robins =   subgenus *Trillium*

   1. Western species, flowers white to pink.   2.

    2. Leaves with petioles to 1" long.   *T. rivale*

    2. Leaves sessile.   3.

     3. Rhizomes elongate, branched.   *T. hibbersonii*

     3. Rhizome stout, unbranched.   *T. ovatum*

   1. Species east of Great Plains. Flowers white, pink, red, purple, rarely yellowish.   4.

    4. Leaves with petioles 3 - 15 mm (3/5") long.   5.

     5. Flowers nodding, usually pink.   *T. catesbaei*

     5. Flowers erect, white.   6.

      6. Petals sharp- pointed, red at base, late flowering.   *T. undulatum*

      6. Petals blunt, all white, may turn pink, early flowering.   *T. nivale*

    4. Leaves sessile.   7.

     7. Flowers nodding beneath leaves.   8.

      8. Flowers red, very large, flared.   *T. vaseyi*

      8. Petals white, strongly recurved.   9.

       9. Petals to 2" L:W = 3:2, anthers twice the filament length.   *T. rugelii*

9. Petals to 1 1/2" L/W = 2:1, anthers = filament length. *T. cernuum*

7. Flowers erect to declining, not consistently nodding. 10.

   10. Rhizome less than 1/2" diameter, whitish. 11.

      11. Rhizome free-branching, colonial habit. *T. pusillum virginianum* etc.

      11. Rhizome cylindric, unbranched, scattered habit. *T. p. ozarkanum* etc.

   10. Rhizome more than 1/2" diameter, brownish, unbranched. 12.

      12. Flowers white, may turn pink. 13.

         13. Leaves and petals broad, leaves L:W = 1:1 14.

            14. Petals broader above middle. 15.

               15. Petals turn pink, pistil green. *T. grandiflorum*

               15. Petals remain white, pistil purple. *T. erectum*

            14. Petals broader below middle, remain white. 16.

               16. Pistil white, large, deep-grooved. *T. flexipes*

               16. Pistil black, 1/2 length of stamens. *T. simile*

         13. Leaves and petals narrow, L:W = near 3:1 *T. persistens*

      12. Flowers purple, yellowish, or beige. 17.

         17. Petals broadest below middle, clasping, recurved,
             pistil concealed from side view. *T. sulcatum*

         17. Petals broadest at or above middle, loosely spreading,
             pistil exposed *T. erectum*

A Survey of Trillium Species
Wake-Robins = Pedunculate Species
Trillium grandiflorum (Michaux) Salisbury
"Showy Wake-Robin"

To many gardeners this species epitomizes the word "Trillium". World-wide, it is the best-known, most widely grown, most pleasing species. It has a large natural range, is extremely variable, easily satisfied in the garden, and readily propagated. Is it any wonder that this species, alone, accounts for most of the garden selections of Trilliums?

Well-grown plants average 10-12 inches tall, but may reach 18 inches (45cm). They grow from stout rhizomes about 2 x 5 cm. They require about 5 to 6 years after germinating to reach flowering size. Encircling scars, along the rhizome, mark the annual procession of terminal, protecting sheaths discarded as each new flowering shoot expands in April or May. Two or three sheath rings separate successive stalk scars. The conical terminal bud rejuvenates each Spring just ahead of the current season stalk attachment. Within the bud a primordium for the following season's bud is already present. The broad, sessile leaves may be over 6" (15cm) long and wide, tapering to a point, and uniform rich-green in color. Large flowers are held erect on slender stalks from less than 1 to more than 4 inches long (2-11cm). The pointed, light-green sepals can vary from less than one to over 2 inches long, and about one-third as wide. The large, showy petals are white as they open but usually turn pink, and may be dark rose as

they ripen. They may attain a length of over 3 inches (8cm) and half that width. They are broadest toward the end, and rather rounded, but with a mucro point. Aberrant forms may have smaller, narrower petals and leaves. Stamens are slightly longer than the 6-ridged, pale green pistil. Yellow anthers are 5-16 mm, and white filaments are 2-13 mm long. The 3 slender stigmas are 3-18 mm long. Ripe fruits are green, 6-ridged, ovate to globular. As with all American Trillium species, the chromosome number 2n=10.

Trillium grandiflorum grows wild from Quebec and Ontario through New Hampshire, Vermont, Connecticut, Massachusetts, New York, New Jersey, Pennsylvania, and south to the Carolinas, Georgia, Tennessee, Iowa, Kansas and Minnesota. Throughout, it is largely restricted to deciduous woods. It is tolerant of a wide variety of garden conditions, so long as there is adequate soil moisture in Spring, humus-rich soil, and mid-day shade on mature plants. As plants emerge in cool Spring, they thrive in full sun, but benefit from expanding-canopy shade in Summer. Where rainfall totals 50 inches or more per year, these plants will show their appreciation for an occasional top dressing of dolomitic lime and balanced granular fertilizer.

Numerous variants of this species have been described by both taxonomists and horticulturists. In the early 1900s Brother Marie-Victorin described:

Forma *chandleri* - a leafless form with smaller normal, or greenish petals
Forma *lirioides* - leaves distinctly petioled
Forma *polymerum* - leaves, sepals, petals etc. in 4 s or 5 s.

About the same time Louis - Maries described:
Forma *elongatum* - with lance-elliptic leaves, and narrow, lance-shaped petals.
Forma *dimerum* - only 2 each leaves, sepals, petals, and carpels.
Forma *striatum* - petals striped green and white.
Forma *petalosum* - all stamens and carpels converted to white petals = 12 or more.

Forms described by others include:
Forma *viride* Farwell - petals all green.
Forma *parvum* Gates - smaller, flowers turn pink soon after opening, Vermont, New Hampshire, Illinois.
Forma *variegatum* Smith - petals with green sectors, often malformed.
Forma *roseum* - petals turn strong pink promptly after opening.

In response to these names Dr. Fernald commented that this is teratology (study of freaks) not taxonomy.

Only a few have been propagated under cultivar names:
'Green Mutant' - green petals edged white.
Doubled forms have been collectively called "Flore-pleno".
'Snow Bunting' - a fine double white with about a dozen petals from Ontario Botanic Gardens.
'Eco Double Gardenia' - an informal, many-petaled, full, white double, shading pink eventually.
'Variety Plena' - found near Rochester, N.Y. by W.A. Smith, was shared with henry Teuscher of the Montreal Botanic Garden, who propagated, and distributed plants to others.

Trillium grandiflorum, throughout its range, is prone to reveal scattered specimens with varying degrees of green striping, green sectors, or all green petals. In some colonies nearly all plants reveal some sectoring; in others very few specimens exhibit the trait. While this feature undoubtedly occurs in many species, it has rarely been reported except by Edith Dusek in *T. ovatum*. Occasionally, petal malformation accompanies the green sectors. a similar malformation, and green sectoring is sometimes observed in purple sessile Trilliums, such as *T. cuneatum*. The green sectoring has been attributed to the presence of mycoplasmas, virus-like obligate-parasites, associated with chloroplast formation in normally pigment-free tissue. Random distribution of the mycoplasma in flower primordia cells produces the sectors as the petals develop. It has been suggested that the condition is infectious, and pathogenic, and that such plants should be destroyed. These green-sectored flowers have been observed in unusual frequency in the Great Lakes region, from Michigan to western Pennsylvania and New York. Bob Goplerud, in Michigan, reported collecting many of these specimens, and growing them in his garden for years. The nature of the sectoring in the individuals varied from year to year. In some instances sectoring disappeared, and did not reappear in those plants in subsequent years. He reported normal white-flowered clumps growing in association with green-streaked plants in his garden for more than 10 years without acquiring streaked flowers. Further studies would seem in order, since a lethal response to green-sectoring in Trilliums has not been established.

Trillium grandiflorum, though highly variable, is easily distinguished from other species, and shows little propensity to hybridize. Since it is one of the most planted, and, consequently, most collected from the wild, it is high time for propagators to select superior clones, and increase propagation of this fine garden plant. To this end, Dr. Richard Lighty, of Mt. Cuba Research Center in Greenville, Delaware, has selected an unusual self-propagating clone that he christened 'Quicksilver'. this cultivar freely produces abundant side shoots, year after year. Conceivably this could be the nucleus of a breeding program for superior forms. Dr. Lighty collected this clone in 1958 near Carbondale, Pennsyvania, and registered the cultivar in June, 1992. In Delaware it flowers between April 25 and May 25.

Exciting pigmented cultivars are likely to eventually become available. In the northeastern part of its range, *Trillium grandiflorum* populations often produce deep-pink-flowered individuals, or colonies. Occasionally the anthocyanin pigment develops throughout the above-ground plant body. Leaves, stem, and sepals, as well as the petals, are suffused with purple or red.

For several decades Fred and Roberta Case of Saginaw, Michigan have diligently sought out unique forms of most Trillium species. They have gathered a particularly outstanding collection of *Trillium grandiflorum* plants. Fred reports being led by a student to a woodland site in Michigan rich in double-flowered Showy Wake-Robins. They located 37 distinct double plants of varying characteristics. One of Fred and Roberta's most outstanding clones is a starburst double, with abundant petals,

arranged in six stacks, and decreasing in sizes as they progress toward the center of the flower. They are growing nearly 20 different doubles. Hopefully, some of these fine plants will eventually find their way into propagation, and distribution. None are currently available.

It cannot be overemphasized that full doubles cannot be seed-propagated, because they produce no seeds. Stamens and pistils have been replaced by petals. But they obviously arose from seeds. Therefore, if doubles are prominent in a wild colony, it is likely, that if enough seedlings are grown from that colony, some doubles will appear.

While self-pollination is common among Trilliums, some insect-pollination does occur. Bees visit some species, and flies are attracted to others. In a rich woodland in western North Carolina where *T. grandiflorum*, *T. erectum*, *T. rugelii*, *T. vaseyi*, and *T. undulatum* were all present, swallowtail butterflies were observed busily visiting only *T. grandiflorum*.

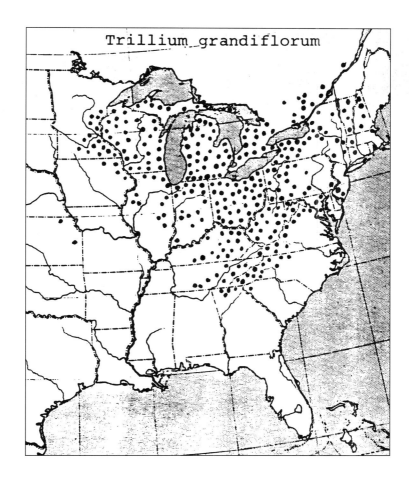

Trillium grandiflorum,Rose Form
photographed by Dr. Mc Clements at the
Royal Botanic Garden in Edinburgh.

Trillium grandiflorum
Superior form.

Trillium grandiflorum
dark form.

Trillium grandiflorum
with green sectors.

Trillium grandiflorum
'Eco Double Gardenia'

Trillium Ovatum Pursh

"Western Showy Wake-Robin"

From the coastal forests of central California, north to Vancouver and British Columbia, across the Cascades to the Northern Rockies in Idaho, Montana, and Wyoming may be found the Western counterpart of *Trillium grandiflorum*. A few isolated colonies of *Trillium ovatum* also occur in the Colorado Rockies. This far-ranging species is fully as variable as its Eastern counterpart. While often found among deciduous vegetation, it is obliged to coexist in open stands of conifers that dominate the area. It flowers from late Febrary in the south to May in the north.

Smooth stems arising from stout rhizomes bear sessile, sharp-pointed, rhombic-ovate leaves that may be up to 6 inches long by 5 inches wide (15cm x 12 cm). Flower stalks are erect and may be from half to nearly 4 inches long. Sepals are lanceolate, acute, and up to 2 inches long (4.5 x 2 cm). Petals are lanceolate to ovate up to 2 1/2 inches long (to 6 x 3 cm), and white turning pink or rose. Stamens are longer than the pistils (8-24 mm). Anthers are yellow, and longer than filaments. Pistils are yellowish-white (6-22 mm long), and prominently 6-winged. Fruit is shallowly 6-winged, green.

Edith Dusek of Graham, Washington, has devoted much of her life to studying this species. She has found and photographed countless variants. Her father named a superior double form (discovered in 1968) 'Edith'. Son, Mark, is propagating this cultivar. Some attractive double forms are being maintained in several botanical gardens in Washington and Oregon. A very nice double named 'Barbara Walsh' is in the Leach Botanic Garden in Portland. It was found in 1957 by Georgia Betz and Doris Weissensluh along Johnson Creek at Barbara Walsh Road. It opens as a multipetaled, flatish, white flower with a red-purple eye, turns cream, and then deep purple.

Edith reports finding numerous green-sectored plants, as have been described from *T. grandiflorum* in the East. She reports on the erratic behavior of these specimens. A plant may display the character one year, and not the next; it may appear in only one or two shoots in a clonal clump; sectored specimens produce normal fruits; no spread to adjacent plants, nor lethal effects have been observed. These observations are relevant in light of claims to the contrary from observations of *Trillium grandiflorum* green-sectored specimens purportedly infected by mycoplasmas, which are considered infectious and lethal, requiring destruction of carrier plants. Apparently this is debatable.

In the garden, equally choice specimens of *T. ovatum* and *T. grandiflorum* are difficult to distinquish. I usually detect a pleasant minty fragrance from *T. ovatum*, and no fragrance from *T. grandiflorum*. The latter often has unusually large sepals, sometimes rather floppy, and the pistil is greener, not so bleached looking. Of course, much of this is academic, because these two species know wher they belong, and when geographically interchanged, they seldom thrive equally.

I know of no efforts at hybridizing these two species, but the effort seems reasonable, and with careful selection might yield some desirable fragrant offspring. Unlike *T. grandiflorum*, *T. ovatum* is known to fraternize in the wild. *T. rivale* x *ovatum* 'Del Norte' was named for the northernmost California county where it was discovered. In British Colombia, apparent intergrades with *T. hibbersonii* have been observed.

Since patterned leaves are virtually unknown among pedunculate Trilliums, a colony of *T. ovatum* in northern California with black-splotched leaves is noteworthy. These plants are otherwise quite typical for the species.

In Washington and Oregon, flowering *T. ovatum* is often accompanied by rambling pink *Dicentra formosa*, yellow Redwood Violets, sweet-smelling Calypso Fairy Slippers, Disporum, and False-Solomon's-Seal.

A cultivar of debated origin and character is being grown both on our West Coast and in England: 'Kenmoor'- in England is known as a full double pink *T. ovatum* that fades to white. Edith Dusek describes it as a flat double white from the University of Washington Arboretum.

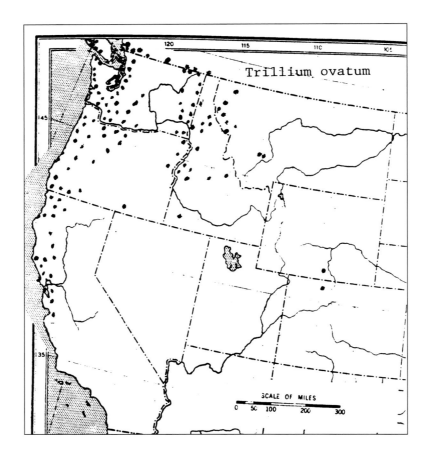

Trillium ovatum

SCALE OF MILES
0   50   100   200   300

T. ovatum in Oregon

T. ovatum in Oregon

A specimen that has
turned pruple due to
injury below ground.

49

T. ovatum 'Barbara Walsh' on opening (L), and later (R), photographed at
Leach Botanic Garden in Portland, Oregon by Matt Bishop of England.

Trilliums hibbersonii Wiley

"Western Dwarf Wake-Robin"

T. hibbersonii in Dusek Garden in Washington.

In rugged woodland on remote portions of Vancouver Island, and British Columbia, this miniature grows in colonies from horizontally branching rhizomes. It has been considered by some to be a diminutive form of *T. ovatum*, but this is no more reasonable than linking *T. pusillum* and *T. grandiflorum*. Actually these Eastern and Western miniatures, often no more than 4 inches (10cm) tall, share many features beside size. Both have branching rhizomes, sessile leaves, pedunculate flowers changing form white to pink, ruffled petals, and seeds that germinate the first season.

I foresee a time, not too distant, when this charming little rock plant will become more readily available. It is now very rare, but it seems more prolific than most species in propagation. It is better known in Europe than in North America at present. Seedlings can develop quite rapidly, usually flowering in three to four years. Plants in mainland British Columbia populations average larger than Island plants. This may indicate introgression of *Trillium ovatum* genes. It is likely that superior, brighter pink cultivars can be bred from these.

Trilliums nivale Riddell

"Snow Wake-Robin"

From Southern Minnesota, Michigan, Ontario, and Massachusetts south to West Virginia, Kentucky, Missouri, and Nebraska, this neat, little, ground-hugging plant, grows in widely scattered, but sizeable colonies. Its range extends all along the gravelly terminal moraines left by retreat of the last continental glaciers. They occupy stabilized old flood plains, as well as wooded hillsides in calcareous soils.

The stubby rhizomes, with few stem scars, indicate unusually fast absorption and disintegration of older rhizome reserves. The smooth stems average 3-4 inches long. The ovate leaves, with blunt tips, seldom exceed 2 x 1 inch (5 x 3 cm), with petioles to 1/2 inch long. In some populations the leaves are a stealy blue-green. The white flowers can be large for the size of the plant, with blunt, obovate petals nearly 2 inches long (to 45 x 20 mm). The blunt sepals are up to 30 x 7 mm. The stamens with yellow anthers are about as long as the pale green pistil. After pollination, the rather smooth globose pistil disappears under the leaves, as the erect, to 1 inch long, peduncle suddenly bends downward. This is a constant, and unique feature in this species, and may have survival value.

Flowering occurs from mid-March to May, depending on Spring-thaw conditions, and it is not uncommon for the plant to be covered by late snows which do it no harm. At Eco-Gardens it ripens off by early June, earlier than most species. A semi-exposed site that is very moist in Spring, and calcareous soil pleases it in the garden.

51

T. nivale Southern Ohio.

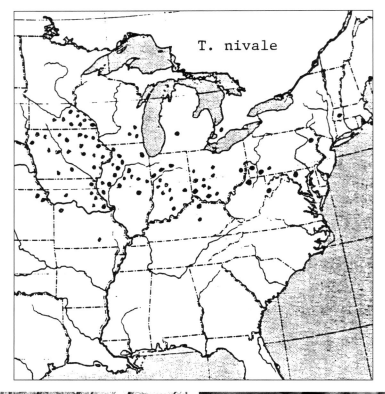

52

T. nivale habitat and natural group photographed in southern Minnesota by Dr. David Vesall.

Trillium Pusillum Complex

"Dwarf Wake-Robin"

Carolina Dwarf = *pusillum*,   Sessile Dwarf = *virginianum*,   Mountain Dwarf = *monticulum*
Ozark Dwarf = *ozarkanum*, Texas Dwarf = *texanum*, Alabama Dwarf = *alabamicum*
Georgia Dwarf = *georgianum*, Kentucky Dwarf = *kentuckianum*

A similar but diverse group of small Trilliums is scattered from East Texas, and the Ozarks of Arkansas and Missouri, to the coastal forests of Maryland, Virginia, and the Carolinas. They usually occur in isolated, small but dense colonies. In pre-glacial time, these plants probably were more integrated with a more continuous distribution east to west, and extending well north of their present populations. Since retreat of the glaciers, they have not regained glaciated territory, nor have they expanded from local refugia, and present distributions are greatly fragmented. There is sufficient diversity among them to readily recognize different taxa, but due to limited overview, they have been relegated by taxonomists to a state of confusion.

When in flower, all individuals share sufficient traits to readily recognize them as members of a common group. All have white, ruffle-edge petals that turn rose-pink, and are approximately the length of the sepals. All have small, pale-green, ovoid pistils, with little evidence of ridges. All have stamens about equaling the pistil in length, and with yellow anthers on pinkish filaments. Most are early-flowering in March, but Ozarks plants bloom about 2 weeks later, in early April. Until the present work, efforts at separating the various populations taxonomically have relied on floral, foliage, and stature characters. Rhizomes have been ignored This is unfortunate, because valuable diagnostic features exist below ground, and some of these impact the growth habit observed above ground. Lumped measurements of above ground parts of T. pusillum specimens from all parts of the broad range yield quite continuous series of numbers for height of 3 - 12 inches, flower stalks of 0 - near 2 inches, petal length from 1/2 to 1 1/2 inches, and leaf-lengths from 1 to 3 1/2 inches. The ranges of measurements for each population are more resticted, but overlap is too great to allow easy separation on these criteria alone.

An obvious feature of many Dwarf Trillium populations is a dense colonial habit. This is related to freely-branching rhizomes in which the terminus supports a three-leaved flowering shoot, back of which are new branches with simple leaves, older branches with non-flowering triplet leaves, and 2 or 3-year-old branches with flowers. This describes th taxa: *virginianum*, *pusillum*, *georgianum*, and *texanum*, all with slender rhizomes, 1/4 inch or less thick. The rhizomes of Ozarks plants are vastly different. They are unbranched cylinders of congested nodes, to 1/2 inch thick. Unless injured, they seldom produce offshoots. A characteristic feature is their stout, accordioned, contractile roots, but they produce slender branching roots as well. The previously described group often possess only slender roots.

Two taxa recognized here (*alabamicum &
kentuckianum*) share features with the two
previous types. Their rhizomes attain a thickness
of 1/2 inch and may remain unbranched for a
time, but in favorable conditions, vigorous
plants develop prominent internodes, and
produce abundant offshoots, as well as
contractile roots. In drier, rocky sites they may
occur as scattered plants, but in rich mesic sites
they are found in dense colonies. In contrast,
Ozarks plants characteristically occur as
scattered individuals from seedlings, except
where damaged rhizomes have produced little
clusters of offshoots.

The name *kentuckianum* is proposed here
for the first time for plants included with Ozarks
populations by some taxonomists, but occuring
east of the Mississippi River in central
Kentucky, and north-central Tennessee. The
more vigorous of these and the Ozarks
populations attain the largest dimensions found
in the complex. They may reach 10 inches in
height, with flower stalks over one inch, and
petals to 1 1/2 inch long, but the Kentuky
plants may be readily separated by the
proliferating rhizomes and resulting colonial
habit. A surprising *ozarkanum* type population
occurs in central Tennessee.

The name *alabamicum* was applied by John
Freeman to plants in northeastern Alabama,
southeastern Mississippi, and southeastern
Kentucky. We are also placing some
populations in western North Carolina here.
They have stout, propagating rhizomes, but
small plants, seldom over 5 inches tall, with
flower stalks and petals about one inch long.

Until 1996, no populations of Dwarf
Trilliums were recorded from Georgia. In the
Spring of that year, Georgia Department of
Natural Resources workers, Tom Patrick, Jim
Allison, and Brian Dickman, found a
population in a mucky site in Whitfield County
of northwest Georgia. It appears to be a relict

population, quite unlike any nearby
populations. The plants share some traits with
Texas Dwarf Trilliums. They grow in dense
colonies, from slender, diffuse-branching
rhizomes. Plants are small, to 6 inches tall with
narrow, blue-green leaves about 2 1/2 inches
long and scarcely 1/2 inch wide. Petals and
flower stalks are nearly one inch long. The
relatively broad sepals are about 21 x 9 mm. A
unique feature, is the presence of stomates
(breathing pores) dusted sparsely over the upper
leaf surfaces. These are usually resticted to
under-leaf surfaces. John Freeman was the first
to call attention to this feature in the Texas
Dwarf Trillium, where they are more crowded
than in Georgia plants. Among sessile
Trilliums, Freeman records this feature only in
T. viride. The name *georgianum* is employed
here for the first time, and presently applies
only to the single known Georgia population.
The stomates appear like spects of dust or
pollen to the naked eye. For some, a 10x lens
may be nacessary to detect them.

The Texas Dwarf, *texanum*, is readily
recognized by foliage alone. The firm, slightly
ascending, grey-green leaves appear dusty
because of abundant stomates spread across the
upper leaf surfaces. These plants are known
only from low, moist woodlands in easternmost
Texas, and bordering Louisiana. They are
intermediate in size, 6 to 8 inches tall, with
leaves to 3 x 3/4 inches. Flower stalks are
usually slightly over an inch, and petals slightly
less. The dense colonies from small, branching
rhizomes usually have a small percentage of
flowering individuals.

Actually, the first Dwarf Trilliums collected
and described were sessile-flowered plants
from coastal Virginia recorded in 1743 by
Gronovius. This was not realized until long after
Michaux applied the name *Trillium pusillum to*
pedunculate specimens from the Carolinas in
1803. It was not until 1943, 200 years after the

Gronovius description, that Fernald named the sessile plants *Trillium pusillum* var. *virginianum*. There is little difference between these two varieties other than flower-stalk length, and range location. Both are coastal woodland plants. Variety *pusillum* from North and South Carolina has peduncles from 1/4 to 3/4 inches long, with length tending to increase in southward progression. Variety *virginianumn* from Virginia and Maryland is essentially stalkless but may have peduncles to 1/8 inch long.

In 1982, Bodkin & Reveal separated the sessile-flowered populations in the Shenandoah Mountains of West Virginia and Virginia as var. *monticulum*. These are scarcely distinguishable from *virginianum* structurally, and most taxonomists consider them synonymous. Considering habitat differences, physiological differences may separate them, but we have not had adequate experience with var. *monticulum* to determine this.

All forms of Dwarf Trilliums are charming plants for shady rock gardens, terraces, and woodland trail-sides. All are easy to satisfy in good woodland soils, and all but the Ozark Dwarf rapidly produce pleasing colonies.

KEY TO TRILLIUM PUSILLUM TAXA

A. Flowering rhizomes slender, to 1/4 inch (-7 mm) thick, and freely-branching.   B.
  B. Flower sessile or stalked less than 1/8 inch.   virginianum
  B. Flower on stalk more than 1/4 inch long.   C.
    C. Leaves with stomate pores above.   D.
      D. Leaves ascending, grey-green, and appearing dusty, to 3/4 inch wide.   texanum
      D. Leaves not ascending, blue-green, about 1/2 inch wide.   georgianum
    C. Leaves medium green, without stomates above.   pusillum
A. Flowering rhizomes comparatively stout, to 1/2 inch (-13 mm) thick.   E.
  E. Rhizomes unbranched and with crowded nodes.   ozarkanum
  E. Rhizomes freely branching , and with prominent internodes.   F.
    F. Plants robust, to 8 inches or +, petals to 1.5 inches   kentuckianum
    F. Plants small, to 6 inches, and petals to 1.0 inches long.   alabamicum

55

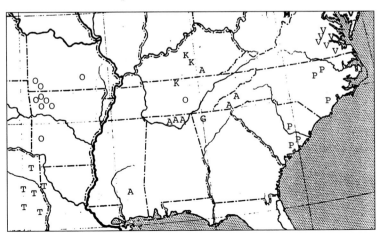

A= *alabamaicum*   K= *kentuckianum*   O= *ozarkanum*   T= *texanum*
G= *georgianum*   M= *monticulum*   P= *pusillum*   V= *virginianum*

T. p. virginianum

T. p. alabamicum

56

T. p. georgianum

T. p. ozarkanum

Natural propagation
T. lancifolium and
T. p. virginianum

Trillium simile Gleason

"Sweet White Wake-Robin"

This little-known, but distinctive, species is very attractive, and easily identified, in its purest form. Unfortunately, there are many plants that appear to share traits between this, *T. erectum*, and *T. flexipes*, as well as *T. vaseyi*.

Characteristically, this plant has very large, snowy-white, outward-facing flowers with a green-apple fragrance, and a black eye. Its stamens are half again the height of the tiny near-black pistil. Its sessile leaves are broadly elliptic on a glabrous stem up to 18 inches tall from a stout, sculptured rhizome. The large, straight, ovate, flaring petals are up to 55x35 mm. (more than 2 inches x nearly 1 1/2 inches). The light green, lanceolate sepals may be up to 40 x 15 mm. with channeled tips, and are about 1/2 the length of the peduncles.

The name *simile* refers to a resemblance to *T. vaseyi*. Tom Patrick has named a maroon-flowered form of *T. simile* forma *rubrotinctum*.

This is a Blue Ridge Mountain species occurring in rich coves, often with Silver Bell (*Halesia*) and hemlock, from North Georgia into the Smokies. It flowers midseason, mid-April near Atlanta.

Synonyms:

= *T. erectum* var. simile
  (Gleason) Ihara & Ihara

= *T. erectum* var. *vaseyi t. simile*
  (Gleason) Ahles

57

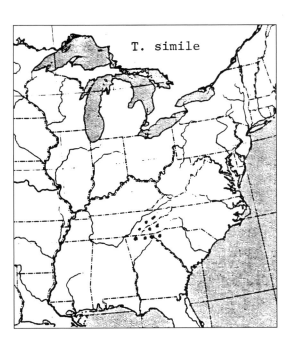

Trillium *simile*

Trillium vaseyi Harbison

"Vasey Wake-Robin"

This is truly a majestic plant. It not only produces the largest of all Trillium flowers (up to 4 inches across), but it is a robust plant with robust company in rich cove forests of North Georgia, Tennessee, and North and South Carolina.

Glabrous stems to 20 inches tall arise from stout sculptured rhizomes, and bear sessile (or very short-petioled) rhombic leaves up to 8 inches long and wide. The huge flowers are usually concealed beneath the large leaves, unless the plant is on an uphill slope from the viewer. Peduncles are from 1-5 inches long. Light green, lanceolate sepals are up to 45x15 mm. with channeled tips. The tips of the very broad petals role back creating a roundish flower. Petals up to 60x45 mm. are usually maroon, but Tom Patrick has named white-flowered specimens forma *elegans*. They may have a rose fragrance. The stamens, with yellow to gray anthers, are about 1.5 x as long as the small, purple, 6-ridged pistil. The purple, ovoid fruits are up to 2 centimeters in diameter.

Trillium vaseyi is sometimes found in company with *T. decumbens*, *T. erectum*, *T.luteum*, *T. simile*, or *T. catesbaei*. It has been known to hybridize with *T. erectum* and *T. simile*.

Henning von Schmelling of the Chattahoochee Nature Center near Atlanta discovered an unusually prolific clone of this species, with four side propagules. When these and the terminal shoot were removed, the stump promptly produced eleven new tubers. Work with this clone continues.

58

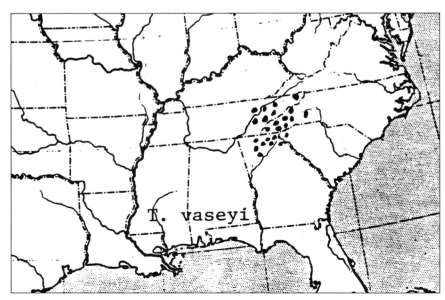

Trillium *vaseyi*

Trillium catesbaei Elliot

"Nodding Rose Wake-Robin"

While quite variable, Trillium catesbaei is a distinctive species with no close relationship with any other species. In its best forms, it is a very attractive, and adaptive garden plant. Most showy forms hold flowers on tall stems beneath the leaves. The leaves are well spaced on petioles, and are more or less rolled upward, exposing the flowers, which may be white, pink, or rose. The least showy forms have rather warped-looking petals, only about 1/3 inch wide, and pale in color, but the better forms have oblong, strongly-recurved, and ruffled petals more than 2 inches long and 1 inch broad. In some poor forms, flowers are held just above the leaves.

Trillium catesbaei is distinctly an upland plant of well-drained oak-hickory woodlands from Virginia through the Carolinas and Tennessee to Georgia and Alabama.

Stout, but unsculptured, rhizomes give rise to smooth, purple stems to 16 inches tall with 5 veined, pointed, ovate leaves to 5 x 3 inches.

Eco Ivory

The leaves may have petioles of 1/2 inch, or slightly longer. Flowers are on stalks 1/2 to 2 inches long, held horizontally or recurved. The lanceolate, green sepals are up to 40 x 14 mm. In small-flowered plants, petals may be quite erect and malformed looking, but in large flowers, the broad, blunt petals are strongly rolled back exposing the bright yellow recurved anthers which extend above the stigmas. The ovary is angular-ovoid and ripens to a globose berry 1/2 inch broad, and greenish. The fragance is unusually variable, from non-descript-earthy to delightful essence of Lilacs, or a pungent liniment odor.

Named cultivars include:

'Eco Rose' - with large ruffled rose-pink flowers.

'Eco Ivory' - large ruffled white that may blush pinkish after pollination.

Synonyms:

Trillium stylosum Nutt.

Trillium nervosum Elliot = a slender form.

T. declinatum Raf. not (A. Gray) Gleason

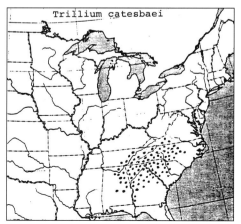

60

Trillium rugelii Rendle

"Southern Nodding Wake-Robin"

On mature flood plains, and moist woods along streams in the Piedmont, and low mountains of the Carolinas, Tennessee, Georgia, and Alabama the Southern Nodding Trillium grows in dense colonies. It closely resembles *Trillium cernuum*, its Northern counterpart, but is a more impressive garden plant. For a basic comparison see the account of *T. cernuum*.

Unfortunately, the accounts in the literature present a far too restrictive, and misleading view of this taxa. The use of characters involving distribution of anthocyanin pigments in flowers to diagnose species is fraught with problems. Some accounts recognize *T. rugelii* by purple pigment at the base of the white petals. The same diagnosis describes the ovary as deep purple, and both anthers and filaments of the stamens as purple. This diffusion of purple anthocyanin pigments to several floral parts is not unusual or surprising. But this description of *T. rugelii* seems to apply only to very rare individuals or local populations. Most populations in Georgia, Alabama, the Carolinas, as well as Tennessee have all white petals, and near-white pistils. Stamens usually are purple to some degree, and this often carries to the top of the pistil. Ripening fruits are usually greenish with purple staining, have 6 well-spaced ridges, and are up to 2 cm. broad. They may contain up to 60 light brown seeds.

Trillium rugelii can be over 20 inches tall, with large, rhombic, glossy leaves to 8 inches broad in rich damp sites. There may be a statistical difference between the stamens of the Northern and Southern species. Anthers of *T. rugelii* are consistently near twice as long as the filaments, but in *T. cernuum*, anthers and filaments are about equal in length, and the plant averages smaller in all parts than its southern counterpart.

As *T. rugelii* becomes better understood, it is likely that superior clones will find their way into cultivation. In western North Carolina, this species hybridizes with *T. erectum* to yield some exciting plants with large rose to pink nodding or divergent flowers. It may also hybridize with *T. vaseyi*.

Trillium rivale S. Watson

"Siskiyou Wake-Robin"

Flattened by sleet, and scarcely visible beneath sparse, low shrubs, this little Trillium can hardly be considered exciting. But standing proudly erect, in showy groups, in seepage-saturated black soil among rocks, on steep slopes, or among fallen branches on forest margins, *Trillium rivale* is an endearing sight. In the first instance their very presence may be credited to protection from deer-browsing afforded by tough overhanging shrubs. In the second, inaccessibility on steep, wet slopes can be credited.

This very distinctive species occurs only in the Siskiyou Mountains of Southwest Oregon, and neighboring Del Norte County of Northwest California. During flowering its roots are constantly bathed in cool, fresh seepage water, and they probably never completely dry out.

Their horizontally-spreading rhizomes are quite unique. They are somewhat flattened, about 1/2 inch broad, pale in color, with occasional branches, and sometimes clusters of tiny bulbils. Fine brown sheath rings are conspicuous against the shiny white internodes, and the large shoot scars clearly display bundle scars. No other Trillium exhibits these features so clearly. Often the rhizomes are strangely malformed from creeping among talus rocks. Their shallow rhizomes are in stark contrast to the very deep-set bulbs of companion, *Erythronium hendersonii*. On exposed serpentine ledges above them grow wispy *Cheilanthes siliquosa* ferns, and near-by wet pockets may be filled with Cobra Pitcher Plants (*Darlingtonia*).

The prominent petioles, to 1 inch, and peduncles from 1 to 4 inches on a little plant with a purplish stem only 3 to 6 inches tall is unique, as is the delicate fragrance of elderberry flowers. *T. rivale* flowers are usually white with varying prominence of purple flecks, but some fine clear pinks occur. The sharp-pointed, ovate, veiny leaves are often stealy blue-green, and about 60 x 40 mm. Lanceolate sepals are pale green with purple margins, and are up to 18 x 7 mm. Petals are broad ovate to 30 x 20 mm, and spreading. Stamens have yellow anthers, and are about as tall as the pistil. The pistil is up to 12 mm. tall with a creamy white ovary that ripens into a greenish angular-globose berry. It flowers mostly through the month of April with considerable variety.

Cultivars:

'Purple Heart' - a cultivar with unusually prominent purple pattern.

'Eco Pink cherub' - erect, broad-petaled clear pink.

Trillium rivale x *ovatum* 'Del Norte' - a natural hybrid found in Del Norte County, California.

In general aspect, *T. rivale* is reminiscent of the Eastern Painted Trillium, *T. undulatum*. Both have dark, veiny leaves with long points, and prominent petioles. Both have erect peduncles, and often have patterned petals.

Dr. Carl Denton of Leeds, England reports that he has not encountered non-flowering 3-leaved *T. rivale*. Seedlings produce single leaves that increase in size annually until strong enough to produce 3-leaved flowering plants. Most species produce 3-leaved non-flowering plants for at least a year or two before flowering. This observation appears to be valid.

T. rivale 'Eco Pink Cherub'.

A closer view

T. rivale on steep, wet, rocky slope in northern California

Unique rhizome of *T. rivale* with prominent bundel scars in large shoot scars

Trillium undulatum Willdenow

"Painted Wake-Robin"

In the cool air, and cool, acid soil, from Rhododendron thickets, and conifer forests in the mountains of Georgia, northward through mixed forests to the Gaspe' peninsula and Nova Scotia grows one of our most stately Trilliums. This tailored plant is not among the largest species, but it is distinctive in many ways, and has no close living kin. Its leaves are firm and dark with 1/2 inch purple petioles and wavy margins on ovate, pointed blades to 5 x 3 1/2 inches. The smooth, purplish stem, one foot (more or less) tall rises from a thick lumpy rhizome. The showy flower is held erect on a peduncle a bit over an inch long. The slender-pointed lanceolate sepals, to 35 x 11 mm. are green with purple margins. The sharp-pointed, ovate petals with wavy margins are up to 40 x 20 mm (about 1 1/2 inches long). They are characteristically white with red blaze at the base. An unmarked white type has been named forma *enotatum* by Tom Patrick.

Stamens are slightly shorter than the pistil, and have short grayish purple anthers on pinkish filaments. The ovoid creamy-white ovary develops into a bright-red, shiny berry up to 20 x 15 mm.

The Painted Wake-Robin flowers from April in the South to June in the North. In damp, acid humus soil within its native range it is a happy garden plant. Beyond its range it is not easy to please. We have little hint as to the ancestors of this stranger.

It would require a long-time breeding program to establish Painted Wake-Robins in low-land gardens. A suitable Piedmont site could be selected to grow a quantity of seedlings germinated from seed from a southernmost population. Successive generations could then be grown from survivors at the test site. such a program might also produce superior clones, and reveal peculiar preferences of this species.

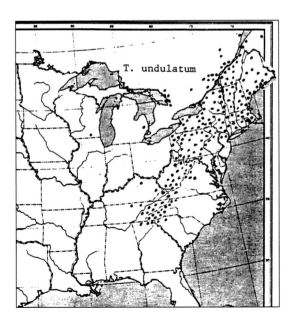

T. undulatum

68

Unusual form lacking ruffles and prominent eye zone.

T. undulatum in fruit among Galax.

T. undulatum

Some cultivars include:

'Eco Gold Star'- tailored yellow petals, yellow anthers, purple ovary, large whitish stigmas with purple midlines.

'Eco Snow-Cap'- pure white, large, lax petals, yellow anthers, dark purple ovary.

'Eco Wine-Cap'- wine-red, large, lax petals, yellow anthers, dark purple ovary.

'Eco Pink Frost'- rose-pink petals, otherwise as above.

Red & white plants togehter in woodland with Spring Beauty.

T. erectum

T. erectum color selections.

'Eco Gold Star'

A bicolor selection

Trillium flexipes Ranfinesque
"Bent Wake-Robin"

Though highly variable, this ancient, wide-ranging species is readily recognized in most of it's populations. It is found from southern Minnesota, Iowa and Missouri, east across southern Wisconsin, Illinois, Michigan, Ohio, Pennsyvania, Kentucky and south through Tennessee to north Alabama and northwest Georgia. It is usually in wet sites, in limestone regions and can attain robust size, but some northern populations consist of rather dapauperate individuals. it is in the ancient deciduous forest heartland, from Kentucky to limestone coves in northwest Georgia, that the Bent Wake-Robin expresses itself most flamboyantly. The very stout rhizomes produce smooth stems to 22 inches tall, bearing sessile, rhombic, pointed leaves to 8 inches broad. The inclined-erect prduncles are up to 5 inches long. Light green, lanceolate sepals sometimes have channeled tips, and are up to 45 x 16 mm. The very large, firm, ovate, white, diverging petals are up to 60 x 30 mm. The long yellow anthers stand about as tall (1 inch) as the large white pistil with its 6-ridged ovoid ovary that develops into a large globose berry to 1 inch diameter. Rarely a bit of purple stains the top of the pistil. A pleasant rose fragrance is characteristic of these plants.

In other populations, peduncles may be horizontal, or declined, even under the leaves, and may be as short as 1 inch or less. Sepals may be much smaller, and petals less than 25 x 6 mm. (1 x 1/4 inch). These plants offer little to attract gardeners, but they usually are easily satisfied in the garden.

In various parts of its range *T. flexipes* grows with or near *T. nivale*, *T. catesbaei*, *T. lancifolium*, *T. grandiflorum*, *T. rugelii*, *T. cernuum*, *T. sulcatum*, and *T. erectum*. Only the latter two appear to have hybridized, in recent time, with the Bent Wake- Robin in the wild. The hybrids with *T. erectum* are often pink to red, and may retain the white ovary of *T. flexipes*, or have pink to purple ovaries, and flowers may be held horizontally or hidden under the leaves. The appearanace of these hybrids can be quite variable, but I fear that the picture has been grossly complicated by lumping with them all the diverse *Trillium sulcatum* forms and hybrids.

Synonyms: =T. declinatum (A. Gray) Gleason
=T. gleasonii Fernald

Cultivars:

'Eco Georgia Giant' - robust plant with erect flowers bearing fragrant creamy white divergent petals up to 60 x 30 mm.

Specimen with declining flower.

Small-flowered Michigan plant.

78

79

T. flexipes in Tennessee woods.

'Eco Georgia Giant'

Trillium persistens Duncan
"Persistent Wake-Robin"

This small, rare species was named for its late-ripening habit. It flowers early in April, and ripens fruits in July, but plants with firm foliage may be found in late August or early September. It occurs only as scattered individuals in mountains in the northeast corner of Georgia and adjacent South Carolina. It is protected as a Federally Endangered Species. It is not a showy garden plant.

The smallish rhizomes, about 1 cm. in diameter, produce slender stems to 10 inches tall with near-sessile, ovate, pointed leaves to 3 1/2 x 1 1/2 inches, that are dark green, with 3 or 5 main veins. Peduncles are usually a little more than an inch long and quite erect. The green, blunt sepals are usually about 21 x 6 mm. The pointed, waxy-margined, white petals to 45 x 15 mm. turn rose with age. Stamens to 15 mm. have 8 mm. yellow anthers that open inward. Greenish pistils are shorter than stamens, and have nearly erect styles and stigmas. Obovate, 6-angled ovaries ripen to berries with persistent styles.

In some flowers the petals do not spread or display well. If seedling populations can be raised, improved strains for rock gardens might be selected and developed.

80

T. persistens

Trillium kamtschaticum Pallas
"Asian Showy Wake-Robin"

This Asian species and its American counterparts, T. ovatum and T. grandiflorum, are scarcely distinguishable, if selected specimens of each are compared. This is the only Asian species with a 2N chromosome number of 10, which is characteristic of all American species. It undoubtedly represents a little-altered modern population, directly descended from Trillium pioneers entering Asia across Beringia from North America. These pioneers undoubtedly were the progenitors of all present Asian Trilliums except *T. govanianum*.

At present, this variable species is found from Kamchatka through the Kuriles to Hokkaido, and northern Honshu in Japan, Sakhalin Island, Amur, and Ussuri in eastern Russia, to northeast China and Korea. Selected cultivars, including doubles, are grown in Japan, but the species is seldom available to American gardeners.

The Asian Showy Wake-Robin grows from a somewhat variable rhizome, usually stout and free of side shoots, but sometimes sprouting quite freely, and sometimes longer and more slender. The smooth, green stems are up to 18 inches tall with pointed, sessile leaves from 2-7 inches broad, and varying considerably in shape. Flowers are held erect on peduncles from 1/2 to over 3 inches. The pale green, pointed sepals vary from 12 - 25 mm. long and 6 - 18 mm. wide, sometimes with channeled tips. Petals are ovate or elliptic, sharp or blunt tipped, from 20 - 60 mm. long by 8 - 35 mm wide, and pure white, not usually turning rose like the American counterparts. Stamens are about equal to the pistil in length, less than an inch, and the anthers are yellow. The conical, green 6-ridged ovary usually has purplish spots, and the mature globose fruit with persistent stigmas, to an inch in diameter, may be purple spotted or all purple.

It would be of interest to attempt hybrid crosses of this and T. grandiflorum. Perhaps this has been achieved in Japan. It flowers from early May to early June, or as late as July in colder regions. It grows in decidous forests with oaks, ash, basswood, elm, birch and on river terraces with alder, willow, and poplar.

Synonym: *Trillium camschatcense* Ker-Gawler

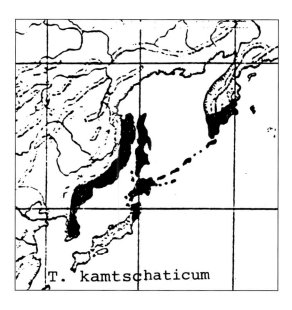

81

T. kamtschaticum

Trillium tschonoskii Maximowicz

"Tschonoski Wake-Robin"

This far-ranging Asian white Trillium must have benefited by its tetraploid innovation (2n = 20 chromosomes) since it occurs from southern Sakhalin south through Japan from Hokkaido to Shikoku, Formosa, Korea, and across China to the Himalayas. It resembles a narrow-petaled *T. kamtschaticum*.

It ha a stout rhizome, and smooth green stem to 18 inches tall with sessile, pointed, rhombic leaves to 7 inches broad. Erect peduncles are up to 2 inches long. Light green lanceolate sepals are up to 32 x 14 mm. The white petals are up to 36 x 18 mm. Stamens and pistils are about equal in length, and smaller than in *T. kamtschaticum*. They are usually not over 13 mm. Anthers are yellow. The 6-ridged, pale greenish, ovoid ovary may have purplish spots or may be all dark purple and fruits are usually greenish and up to 16 mm. broad, but may be dark purple.

Several varieties with purple fruits or flowers of varying proportions, have been described, but they are generally of little horticultural interest.

Synonyms: = *T. morii* Hayata (1910)

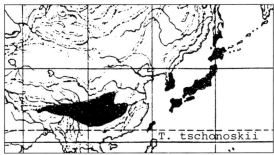

A broad-petaled T. tschonoskii.

A unique black pistil plant.

83

Photos by Dr. J. McClements in Great Britain.

Trillium apetalon Makino

"False-Petal Wake-Robin"

This purple flowered Trillium is something of a fraud. It produces no petals, but the ovate sepals are usually rich purple, although some are greenish purple, and up to 24 x12 mm. They usually persist until fruits are near ripe.

Trillium apetalon grows in deciduous forests with magnolias, maples, oaks, elms, and along stream banks with alders, ash, and willows. It occurs from southern Sakhalin, and southern Kuriles, through all four major Japanese Islands, flowering between late April and late June, depending on latitude.

84

This plant sometimes produces clumps from stout rhizomes. Slender green to purplish stems may be up to 16 inches tall, with sessile, broad rhombic leaves to 6 inches wide. Flowers are held on erect peduncles to

Trillium apetalon

Photo by Dr. J. McClements in Great Britain.

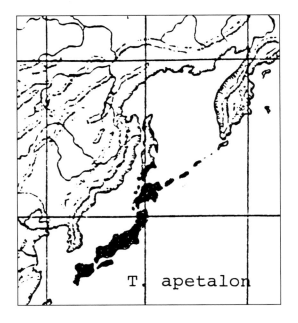

T. apetalon

2 inches long. Stamens and pistils are small, about equal in length, less than 1/2 inch. anthers can be purple or creamy yellow. Ovoid 6-ridged ovaries are green to purple, and the fruits are the same color, and up to 16 mm. broad. The 2n chromosome number is 20.

This species offers no unusual problems in garden culture, but it is grown more as an oddity than a show-piece. Several unusual types have been given varietal names, but no named cultivars are horticulturally available.

Trillium smallii Maximowicz
"Small's Wake-Robin"

This is a strangely variable taxon of hybrid origin that is often compared to, and confused with *T. apetalon*. It is an allopolyploid (2n = 30 chromosomes) between *T. apetalon* and *T. kamtschaticum* - type parents. It has been found only in southern Sakhalin and Hokkaodo, in deciduous forests, on slopes approaching the sea, and flowering in April and May. Like *T. apetalon*, it is purple flowered, and often lacks petals, but it may have three that are nearly circular in outline, and less than one inch in diameter. Also like *T. apetalon*, its persistent sepals are usually purple, to 30 x 14 mm., and may have channeled tips. Stamens and pistils are rather small, about equal in height, less than 1/2 inch. Stamens are usually purple. The 6-ridged greenish ovary, only 9 mm wide, develops into a large, to 27 mm, berry. Small's Wake-Robin has smooth green stems from a large rhizome. Its rhombic, sessile leaves may be up to 7 inches broad with prominent sharp tips. Flowers lacking petals may have 9 stamens, and amomalies such as 2 petals with 7 stamens occur.

The more robust individuals of this Trillium are interesting garden plants, and not difficult to please.

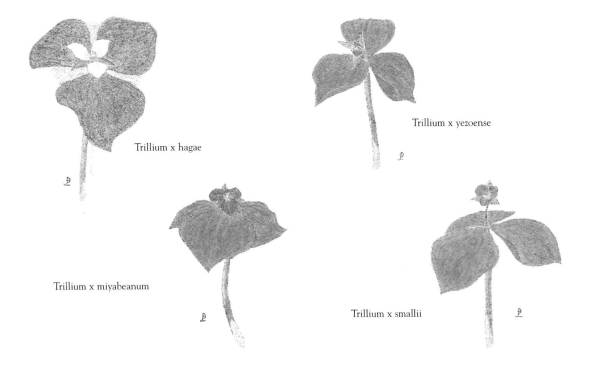

Trillium x hagae

Trillium x yezoense

Trillium x miyabeanum

Trillium x smallii

Trillium hagae Miyabe & Tatewaki
"Hagae Wake-Robin"

This showy, white Trillium of recent hybrid origin has been found only on Hokkaido Island of northern Japan, usually in consort with its parents *T. kamtschaticum* and *T. tschonoskii* in deciduous forests of maples, oaks, elms, etc. It is a fertile allopolyploid (2n=30 chromosomes) arising from parents with 2n=10 and 2n=20 chromosomes respectively. A sterile triploid, *T. x hagae* (2n=15), is often present as well. The large fruits, to an inch in diameter, full of seeds, easily distinguishes the hexaploids from the sterile, smaller-fruit triploids

Smooth green stems rise to 18 inches from large rhizomes, and bear sessile, large, rhombic leaves to 8 inches broad. Erect peduncles to an inch or more support flowers with fairly large green sepals to 40 x 16 mm., and broad-ovate, white petals to 50 x 28 mm. Stamens and pistils are near equal height to about 16 mm. The rather long anthers are yellow and filaments are greenish. Pistils are yellowish green, often with purple near the top, and a 6-ridged conical ovary.

Hagae Wake-Robin could be an attractive garden plant, but it is presently not available to American gardeners. It flowers usually in May.

86

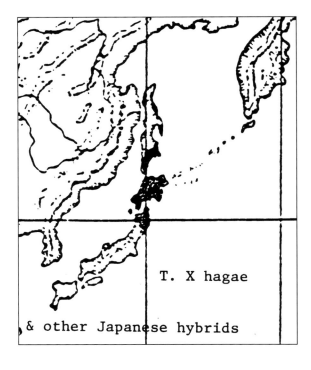

T. X hagae

& other Japanese hybrids

Trillium x miyabeanum
Tatewaki
"Miyabe Wake-Robin"

This sterile hybrid between *T. apetalon* and *T. tschonoskii* is largely of academic interest. It helps to illustrate that all species of Trilliums occurring in northern Japan do hybridize in the wild. The number of stable species is very few, only three, but all possible combinations have been found in recent hybrids

Miyabe Wake-Robin has been found only on Hokkaido and northern-most Honshu in deciduous forests of oaks, maples, elms, ironwood, baswood, and birchs, and usually with both parents present. Both parents, and the hybrid have the tetraploid chromosome number (2n = 20) but genetic differences are so great that viable seeds are not produced.

The sessile, rhombic leaves of this plant are usually large, to 9 inches broad, with sharp, drawn-out tips. Peduncles are 1 to 2 inches long. Sepals are purple-stained, and to 35 x 16 mm. Petals are often absent, but one to 3, broad, purple, to 28 x 23 mm. may be present. Sometimes petals with pollen sacs are present. There are usually six stamens, but occasionally 7 or 8 are present. They are about equal to the pistils in height, and purple with yellowish anthers. The 6-ridged ovary is usually yellowish with purple top and spots. Flowering is usually in May.

Albiflorum - a white - flowered form described by Soukup.

Trillium x yezoense
Tatewaki
"Yezo Wake-Robin"

This sterile, triploid (2n = 15) between *T. apetalon* and *T. kamtschaticum* represents a first generation hybrid equivalent to an earlier hybrid that gave rise to the hexaploid, allopolyploid, *T. smallii* (2n = 30). It has been found only on Hokkaido in company with both parents.

Like *T. smallii* it may lack petals, or have 1 or 2 somewhat-smaller, purple, near-round petals (sometimes with pollen-sacs) to 20 x 18 mm. Erect peduncles are about an inch long. Sepals are usually broader than in *T. smallii*, to 32 x 20 mm. Stamens and pistils are about equal in height, to 10 or 12 mm. Stamens are purplish with yellow anthers. Conical 6-ridged ovaries are yellowish with purple tops, and enlarge only slightly since ovules do not develop. Flowering usually occurs in May.

Synonym: = *T.* x *amabile* Miyabe & Tatewaki

Trillium govanianum Wallich ex Royle
"Himalayan Triplet Lily"

T. govanianum photographed at the
Royal Botanic Garden in Edenburgh
by Dr. J. McClements.

This is a smallish plant, up to 10 inches tall, with moderate size ovate leaves to 3 1/2 x 2 inches on petioles under 1/2 inch long. The firm leaves, with 3 main veins, end in long slender tips. Flowers are born on peduncles a bit longer than 1/2 inch. Sepals and petals are small, purple, and very slender, not more than 18 x 3 mm. The 6 stamens are also very small with yellow anthers about 3 mm. long. The purple ovoid ovary is about 5 x 3 mm. with slender, erect, near-black styles to 6 mm. long, from a disc, and matures into a purple, globose fruit. It usually flowers in May.

While the plant is of modest size, it produces robust rhizomes with abundant offshoots, a rare attribute among Trilliums. It thrives in gardens in Scotland and Southern Sweden, but is seldom encountered in England, and virtually unknown in America.

This hermit of the Himalayas is so different from most Trilliums that it is commonly excluded, and placed in the genus *Trillidium*. It shares its "flower parts in whorls of 3" with all Trilliums, but many of its traits are more allied to the genus *Paris*. It grows at high elevations among Rhododendron and *Abies spectabilis*, at 10 - 12,000 feet, from Kashmir to Bhutan. Some Paris species occur there, but no other Trilliums come close, geographically or genetically. It shares its 2n = 20 chromosome number with only two stable Trilliums, *T. apetalon* and *T. tschonoskii*, but many species of Paris have this number.

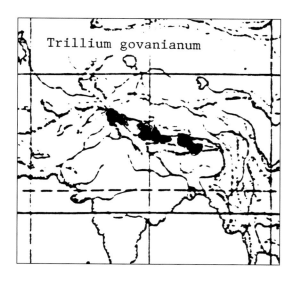

Trillium cuneatum Rafinesque

"Whippoorwill Toadshade" (Sweet Betsy, Bloody Butcher)

Few Trilliums offer the gardener greater variety than this widespread sessile species. Its foliage varies from extravagant marbled patterns, to pure silver green, or uniform dark purple-green. Petals can be broad or narrow, yellow, chartreuse, bronze, or rich maroon, and may approach 4 inches in length. Plants may be very broad-leaved, and stocky, or 20 inches tall, and graceful.

This is probably one of our oldest living Trillium species, genetically not far removed from an early transcontinental population that gave rise to some Western species such as *T. kurabayashii and T. angustipetalum*. Today it occupies a variety of deciduous forest communities from western Mississippi, across Alabama, and north half of Georgia, South Carolina, western North Carolina, Tennessee, and south Central Kentucky. In the South and West portion of its range it is commonly in old flood plain forests. In north Georgia, and north into Carolina and Tennessee mountains, it is on wooded slopes of rich coves.

Trillium cuneatum is an excellent example of innate variability within a species. There is a tendency to suspect hybridization, and look for interlopers when an unusual degree of variation in a population is observed. In old flood-plain woods of the Piedmont, near Atlanta Georgia, this is the only sessile Trillium species present, and its variation is notorious. In the mountains, 100 miles to the north, still another range of variation is exhibited. The very diverse individuals are readily identified by association within these communities, but if isolated variants are analyzed, without reference data, identification could be very difficult. Further, if such an isolate were allowed to self-pollinate into an extended population an instant new taxon would be born.

The Whippoorwill Toadshade is the only sessile Trillium present in most communities in its large range so identity problems are minimal. In marginal areas some confusion can exist. In the southern Coastal Plain of Alabama, Georgia, and South Carolina *T. maculatum* approaches but does not really intergrade. From southern Alabama into central Tennessee *T. stamineum* overlaps the range of *T. cuneatum*, but it flowers later, and it shows no propensity to hybridize with anything. *T. ludovicianum* is a distinct species of central Louisiana, but it has a few populations east of the River in Mississippi where it meets *T. cuneatum* at its southwest extreme. *T. maculatum, T. ludovicianum,* and the Mississippi *T. cuneatum* are all early risers, appearing in mid-February, and in full bloom by early March. In this area, some intergrading is apparent. The greatest overlap and likelihood of confusion is with *T. luteum*, which occurs from north Georgia across eastern Tennessee into southern Kentucky, largely within the gross range of *T. cuneatum*. This is of some concern because *T. cuneatum* commonly produces mixed populations with some yellow individuals. Actually this overlap is more apparent than real, since this is territory covered by the Ridge and Valley Province and Western Appalachia where *T. cuneatum* is largely absent, and neither species occurs on the Cumberland sandstones. In the great Smokies *T. luteum* is the only sessile species among the rich assemblage of pedunculate Trilliums. Nevertheless, there is evidence of hybridization where they mingle in western North Carolina, southern Kentucky, and southern Tennessee.

The stout rhizomes of Whippoorwill Toadshade are usually very conservative, producing only a single stem yearly for many years. After fifteen years in the garden, several plants produced only two or three shoots each. One plant, however had produced a clump of 36 stems in that period of time. Such rapid propagation may, or may not be genetic. Destruction of the terminal bud can induce

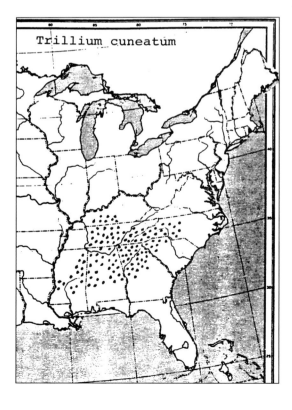

Trillium cuneatum

lateral shoot formation which can continue for several years.

The stems are glabrous green to purplish and 6 to 20 inches tall, with sessile, broad ovate to rhombic leaves to 6 inches long or broad. Leaves are nearly always patterned, but very rarely uniform light silver-green, or dark purple-green plants occur. Marbling is usually in multi-shades of green and near black. Plants with yellow flowers are marbled in lighter tones than purple-flowered plants. The cultivar, 'Eco Spectacular', was selected from the wild in Gwinnett County, Georgia, to be propagated, because of outstanding contrast in a balanced two-color near-black and bright green pattern, plus large deep purple flowers.

Green lanceolate sepals are often purple-stained in dark flowers, and may be up to 60 mm. long. Petals are oblanceolate to obovate, to 90 mm. in the former, to 65 mm. in the latter. Color may be very dark purple, bright maroon, bronze, lime green, light yellow, or golden yellow. Light colored petals often have purple bases. Stamens may be up to an inch long, purplish, with long, yellow to olive lateral anthers, barely overtopped by rounded connectives. Pistils are up to 20 mm. long with an ovoid 6-ridged ovary. They flower March to April. Northern populations flower later even when grown in the garden in Georgia. Flowers have a variable fragrance, sometimes fruity or spicy.

Synonyms:
> = *T. underwoodii* Small, in part.
> = *T. hugeri* Small
> = *T. maculatum* sensu Shaver, not
> *T.maculatum* Rafinesque

Varieties: *T. cuneatum* forma *luteum* Freeman - floral parts free of purple pigment. Petals yellow.

Cultivars:

'Eco Dappled Lemon' - plant not over one foot, leaves broad with multi-tone marbling, petals broad, clear yellow, stamens yellow / green.

'Eco Green Phantom' - total absence of purple anthocyanin pigment. Leaves unmarked silvery-green, broad-ovate, petals long-lanceolate lime-green, stamens green with yellow anthers, stems all green to 16 inches.

'Eco Marbled Lime' - to 16 inches, leaves ovate with bright, light marbling, petals lanceolate, bright, light green.

'Eco Midnight' - leaves dark purple-green, petals lanceolate dark purple.

'Eco Purple Shadows' - dark, multicolored leaves, petals lanceolate, dark purple

'Eco Silver Tiara' - to 16 inches, unmarked silver-green leaves, large deep purple flowers.

'Eco Spectacular' - to 16 inches, boad black and green patterned leaves, large purple flowers.

'Eco Mississippi Gold' - light-marbled leaves and sepals, yellow petals, gold/brown stamens, purple stems. From central Mississippi.

There appears to be a preponderence of broad-petals, broad-leaf plants in north Georgia and neighboring North Carolina. These plants are also usually shorter in stature. Progressing outward from this center the trend seems toward slimmer plants. No statistics have been developed to verify this obvservation.

'Eco Spectacular'

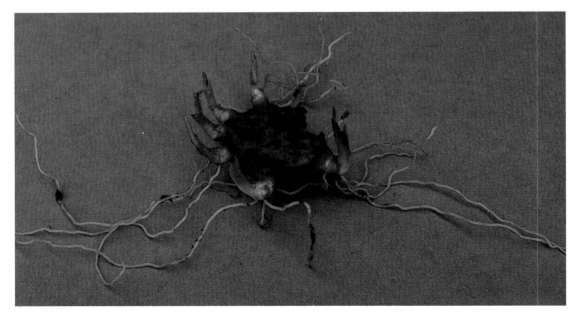

During 16 years in the garden this *T. cuneatum* 'Eco Purple Shadows' underwent no natural vegatative propagation, although the husky rhizome produced 2 or 3 flower shoots annually in later years. When a section of the rhizome was removed, it promptly produced 6 young plants. Notice the different pigmentation in sepals of these sister shoots.

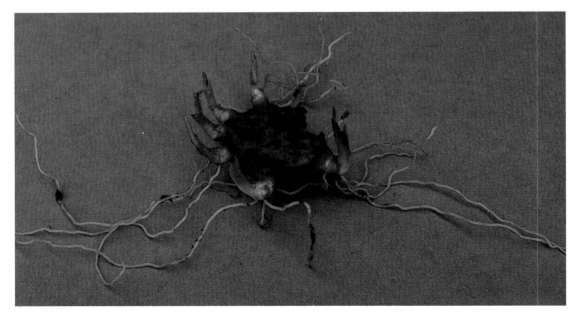

'Eco Mississippi Gold' from central Mississippi.

'Eco Silver Tiara'

93

T. cuneatum 'Eco Green Phantom' from Georgia.

T. cuneatum 'Eco Dappled Lemon'

Trillium luteum (Muhl.) Harbison

"Lemon Toadshade"

This is one, of two, species that produce only yellow flowers, and should therefore not be easily confused with other Trilliums. But this has not been its history.

Synonyms:
- = *T. sessile* var. *luteum* Muhl.
- = *T. underwoodii* Small var. *luteum* (Muhl.) Mac Bride
- = *T. sessile* f. *luteum* (Muhl.) Peattie
- = *T. hugeri* Small f. *flavum* Peattie
- = *T. viride* Beck var. *luteum* (Muhl.) Gleason

It is not unusual to see this fine garden plant illustrated over the name *T. sessile* var. *luteum*. But since there is a distinctive yellow *T. sessile*, now called forma *viridiflorum* Beyer, it is time to clear the record. While there are yellow-flowered individuals of most purple species, only *T. cuneatum* is likely to be confused in the wild. In most cases, the distinct lemon fragrance, total absence of purple pigment in flower parts, modest leaf marbling, and pure colony distribution in mountain coves will identify this species. In the Great Smokies this is the only sessile

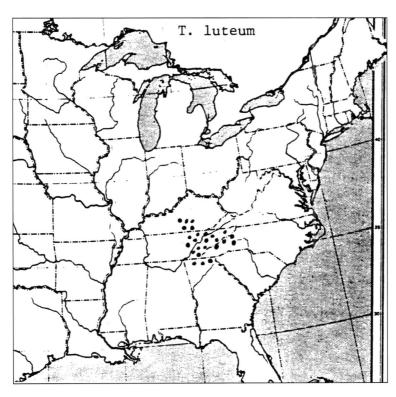

T. luteum

Trillium among the abundant pedunculate forms. Where this and *T. cuneatum* do mingle in western North Carolina, southern Kentucky, and southern Tennessee, there is evidence of hybridization, and some individuals are confusing.

Trillium luteum is found from north Georgia to southern Kentucky and from east Tennessee to extreme western North Carolina, but not on the sandstones of the Cumberland Plateau. Its large rhizomes seldom produce more than one or two stems.

The sessile elliptic leaves may attain 6 inches in length, and the modest marbling may largely disappear by maturity. The green, lanceolate sepals may reach 65 x 17 mm., and the erect, yellow, elliptic petals may attain 90 mm. in length. Anther sacs on the nearly inch long yellow stamens usually open inward. Connective tissue is green. Pistils are shorter than the stamens and have pointed stigmas with recurved tips. Ovoid fruits are yellowish.

96

T. luteum

Trillium stamineum Harbison

"Propeller Toadshade"

This unique Toadshade cannot be confused with any other species. Horizontal, narrow, twisted petals, pilose hairs on the upper stem and under-leaf veins, plus beaked flower buds set this species apart from all others. It is not one of the showiest, but uniqueness, and marbled foliage give it charm.

Its distribution from southern Alabama and bordering Mississippi north into central Tennessee is concise and includes no intergrades or evidence of hybridization. It occurs in rather open oak-pine woods, as well as rich, moist deciduous forest. Flowering occurs from late March in the South to early May in the North.

The stout, rather elongate rhizomes, about 5 x 1.5 cm., have prominent internodes, and are not strongly sculptured. The hairy-topped stems may be green or purple, and to 15 inches tall. Leaves may be prominently or obscurely mottled, often with silvery-green background. On the average, they are ovate to about four inches long. Flower buds usually have small beaks, and are filled with large stamens. Purple-stained, lanceolate sepals, to about 38 mm. long, spread widely. The very narrow twisted petals, to 42 mm. long, spread horizontally. They are usually dark purple to bronze, but may be greenish or yellow, often with purplish bases. The anthers on the large (to one inch) brownish stamens open outward. Pistils are about 1/2 as tall as stamens, with 6 ridged ovary, and recoiled stigmas, often between the anthers. Flowers often have a strong fetid odor, like unbelievaly offensive toe fungus.

forma *luteum* Freeman - yellow petals, no purple in any flower parts.

T. stamineum

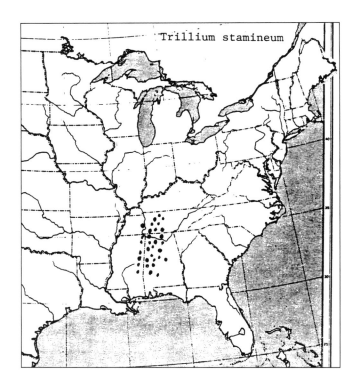

102

T. stamineum

Trillim recurvatum Beck

"Eastern Petioled Toadshade" (Prairie Trillium)

This wide-ranging, stable species is certainly among the oldest living types in the genus. It is amazingly uniform throughout its range, with no evidence of hybridization, and sharing some traits only with *T. lancifolium*. It is likely that *T. recurvatum* had a much greater range prior to glaciation, but in the past 10,000 years it has reoccupied the woodlands of Illinois, Indiana, eastern Iowa, and southern Wisconsin with a vengeance. It continues also southward through Missouri, Arkansas, northern Louisiana, east Texas, northern Mississippi and Alabama, through Tennessee to Kentucky. A surpising relict population occurs in extreme western North Carolina among lime springs in the hills of Madison County

The elongate, but sparsely-branching rhizome, to nearly 5 inches, is unlike any other. It is quite smoothly cylindric to a centimeter, or slightly more, in diameter. In rich sites, it can be quite robust, to 18 inches tall, but usually to 15 inches. The mature leaves have petioles to an inch long. The ovate blades may be up to 7 x 3 inches, weakly marbled at first, but fading to nearly plain green. Lanceolate sepals, to 40 mm. long, recurve abruptly to vertical on opening, but return to near horizontal after pollination. Petiolate leaves allow freedom of movement of sepals. Ovate, stalked petals to 50 x 20 mm. have tips bowed inward. They are usually maroon or bronze, but can be greenish or, rarely, pure yellow. Stamens, to 18 mm. long, have tips bowed inward, and anthers open inward, with connectives extending noticeably above the anthers. Pistils are shorter than stamens, and the 6 wings of the ovary project between the stamen filaments. The fruit is prominently winged.

From South to North, flowering progresses from mid-March to mid-May. It is not surprising to find that this plant with such wide distribution is easily pleased in the garden.

Synonyms:
= *T. unguiculatum* Raf.
= *T. unguiculatum* Nutt.
= *Phyllantherum recurvatum* (Beck) Nieuwl.
= *Trillium reflexum* Clute

103

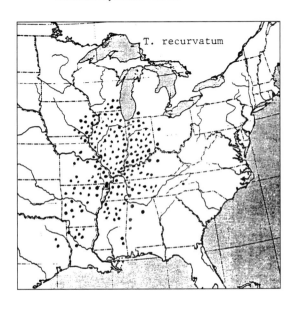

Varieties:

forma *esepalum* Freeman & Heinecke - some small populations of plants without sepals in central Tennessee. Petals, stamens, and pistils in these plants are usually quite normal.

forma *luteum* Friesner - total absence of purple in flower, petals clear yellow. = 'Shayi'

Other names for various freaks have been proposed, but there has been little acceptance or use of them.

Cultivar 'Shay's Yellow'.

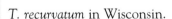

T. recurvatum in Wisconsin.

Plants in fruit with elevated sepals.

A typical long, cylindric smooth rhizome, and fruit.

Trillium lancifolium Rafinesque

"Lance-Leaf Toadshade"

This little Toadshade has probably lost most of its territory to Old Man Cotton. It presently holds out in old wooded flood-plains, and rocky wooded slopes surrounded by old fields in various stages of use, abandonment, and reuse. These sites are widely scattered from the north Florida, Georgia, Alabama intersect, the Fall Line belt across Georgia and South Carolina, to the limestone areas of northwest Georgia and adjacent Tennessee, and a few sites in north Alabama. Despite the efficient vegetative propagation by horizontal, elongate, branching rhizomes, this graceful Trillium is seldom abundant anywhere.

It is consistently linked with *T. recurvatum* in comparative studies, and they may have had a common ancestor, but there is no problem in distinguishing them. The leaves of *T. lancifolium* are always more distinctly patterned than those of *T. recurvatum*, and despite their narrow blades, they often exhibit a silvery-green blaze down the midrib, bordered by dark splashes, as is common in many Coastal Plain Trilliums. Both species have rather slender, elongate, horizontal rhizomes, but the comparison largely ends there. *T. lancifolium* rhizomes are about a third thinner (to 8 mm. diameter), and freely-branching, producing dense colonies. *T. lancifolium* sepals reflex to horizontal or slightly lower, not to a vertical position between petioles (*T. lancifolium* leaves are sessile) as in *T. recurvatum*.

T. lancifolium 'Eco Slim'

T. lancifolium has slender, glabrous, purplish stems to about a foot tall. In different populations the leaf width varies from 1:4 to 2:5 compared to length. Petals are very narrow to 45 mm. long with the lower third reduced to a stalk. Petals are maroon, bronze or greenish or bicolored. Stamens are to 15 mm. long with short anthers opening inward. Incurved connectives project above the anthers. Ovaries have 6 wings projecting between the filaments. The berry is prominently winged.

Synonyms:

= *T. recurvatum* var. *lanceolatum* S. Watson

= *T. lanceolatum* Boykin ex S. Watson

= *T. recurvatum* sensu Chapman

Cultivars:

'Eco Slim' - linear purple flowers, narrow marbled leaves about 1:4 width: length. Stem to 9", leaves to 3 x 3/4'.

106

'Eco Robust' - stem to 12", leaves to 3 3/4" x 1 5/8", flowers bronze, leaf pattern subdued.

'Eco Robust'

Trillium sessile L.

"Common Toadshade"

Our basic-type Toadshade nearly disappeared from modern botanical literature as a result of taxonomic abuse. Thanks to the diligence of John Freeman (1974), we now have reasonable perameters for this widespread species of considerable age, as well as for numerous taxa confused with it.

Except for southern Wisconsin populations of *T. recurvatum*, *T. sessle* is the northernmost sessile species, east of the Rockies. A large part of its distribution is in the terminal moraine hills south of the Great Lakes from eastern Illinois, across Indiana, central Kentucky, Ohio, to western New York, and Pennsylvania, but also through West Virginia to Maryland, and scattered populations in Virginia, and central Tennessee. A surprising relict population occurs in extreme western North Carolina, among lime springs in the hills of Madison County. West of the Mississippi it is scattered through Missouri, northern Arkansas, and eastern Kansas. The southernmost population is recorded in Limestone County in northern Alabama. This species has a distinct east-west distribution with little attempt to break the 35 or 43 north latitude barriers. It probably occurred far north into Canada, but little farther west, prior to glaciation. Southward it can flower in late March, northward it may wait until mid May.

As we might expect, with such a broad range, the Common Toadshade is variable, and grows in a variety of habitats. It joins, *T. flexipes*, and *T. nivale* in some old flood plains, and also occurs in rich upland coves, especially in calcareous areas.

This is not among the most robust species. It grows from a stout, but modest-size rhizome, with stems seldom more than 10 inches tall, and elliptic leaves seldom larger than 4 x 3 inches. Leaves usually unfold with indistinct dark marbling that disappears later. Lanceolate sepals are sometimes purple-stained. Petals vary considerably from narrow to broad elliptic, from 45 x 10 to 35 x 14 mm., and from maroon to bronze, green, or yellowish. Stamens are large with yellowish anthers to 12 mm. opening inward, and connectives extending 3mm. or more above. Pistils are

107

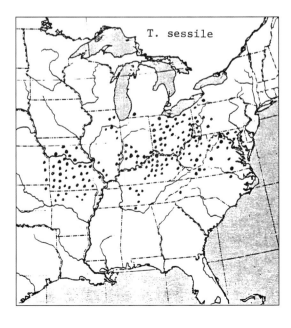

T. sessile

nearly as long as stamens with a 6-winged ovoid ovary about 1/2 as long as stigmas. The broad fruit is distinctly angled. Flowers may have a spicy odor.

The absence of *T. sessile* from most of the State of Illinois is puzzling. Abundant populations west of the Mississippi show some digression from more eastern plants. They average somewhat taller with narrower, more pointed leaves.

Varieties:

forma *viridiflorum* Beyer - petals yellow-green, stamens greenish to purplish, ovary green.

Synonyms:

= *Trillium longiflorum* Raf. = *T. rotundifolium* Raf.

= *T. isanthum* Raf. = *T. tinctorium* Raf.

= *T. membranaceum* Raf.

= *T. sessile* var. *boreale* Nutt.

Cultivars:

'Eco Broad Maroon' - petals wide maroon-purple, stem to 8 inches, leaves broad, slightly marbled, until pollination.

Trillium sessile 'Eco Broad Maroon' from Ohio.

Trillium decipiens Freeman
"Deceptive Toadshade"

There is no more handsome garden plant in this genus than the Deceptive Toadshade. "Deceptive" only because it escaped detection and naming as a distinct species fo so long. Like alll species it exhibits considerable variation, but unlike most, all individuals are remarkably attractive. Its large, richly-colored flowers are unusually long-lasting, but the true beauty resides in its leaves, displayed 15 inches, or more, high on purple stems. The sessile, sharp-pointed, symmetric, ovate leaves display a long-lasting richness of color seldom equaled. From tip to base along the midrib is an irregular silvery band, bordered on both sides by multicolored splotches of dark purple, dark green, and light green. For about four months the display is a traffic stopper. Only its close kin can compete with it for beauty. *T. ludovicianum* is very similar but smaller, and *T. underwoodii* has similar size and color, but is squat, near the ground, and ripens off earlier. Actually, its stems, like those of *T. decipiens*, continue to elongate for a time, lessening the appearance of "squatness".

Lanceolate sepals may reach 3 inches, and are wide spread, often revealing purple streaking, or subdued leaf-like patterns. Petals are oblanceolate, erect, to 3 or 4 inches, and range in color from dark maroon-purple to bronze, and yellow, or bicolor, purple and green. Purplish stamens are up to an inch long, with lateral, yellow anthers and shortly extended connectives. Pistils are about 2/3 the stamen length, with a 6-ridged elipsoid

109

T. decipiens woodland in southern Alabama.

ovary to 15 mm., and stigmas recurved to the ovary. Flowering occurs throughout March, but not until April in northern gardens.

T. *decipiens* is a quite rare plant of limited range from the panhandle of Florida up the Chattahoochee Valley in alabama and Georgia, and across, below the Fall Line to a few sites in Georgia and Alabama, where it sometimes occurs with *T. maculatum*. Some Central Georgia specimens approach *T. underwoodii* in character.

Cultivars:

'Eco Art Work' - large, deep purple flowers, and outstandingly brilliant leaf pattern with silvery mid-stripe, stems are purple.

'Eco Seafoam' - broad chartreuse-yellow petals. Leaves with silver mid-stripe separating multi-tone green marbling. Stems are green.

110

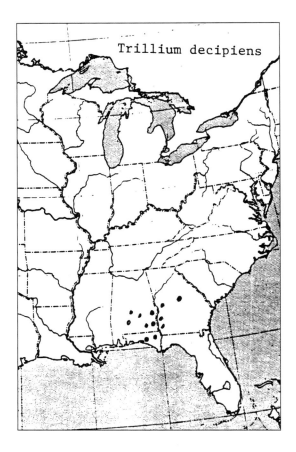

Trillium decipiens

'Eco Seafoam'

'Eco Artwork'

Trillium underwoodii Small
"Underwood's Toadshade"

What has already been said about the beauty and garden-worthiness of T. decipiens may be echoed for Underwood's Toadshade. It has comparable large, deep-colored flowers, and very similar multicolored leaves. It also has a similar small distribution range from north Florida into southern Alabama, and southwest Georgia. Flowering is prolonged from early March into April. Plants at Eco-Gardens in Atlanta are usually up in late January, but flowers are not fully open until early March, whereas populations from which these came, in southwest Georgia, are not usually full open until late March. This may be accounted for by earlier cold conditioning to break dormacy. By contrast, in the far North, in Michigan, this very early riser is one of the last to appear, usually not before May

The large, stout rhizomes of T. *underwoodii* produce smooth stout stems that elongate to about 8 - 10 inches. the multicolored leaves often have a conspicuous silvery blaze the length of the midrib, bordered by rich marbling. Sometimes the pattern is less symmetric, with indiscriminate splotching. They are pointed with rounded bases, and may be up to 6 x 4 inches. The 2 inch sepals are spreading with recurved tips, and may have

Trillium underwoodii 'Eco Decorated Giant'

purple stained bases. Petals to 4 inches long, vary in width up to an inch, and vary in color from dark maroon and bronze to greenish yellow. Stamens, about 3/4 inch long, are purplish with lateral yellow anthers slightly exceeded by the connectives. Purplish pistils are about 2/3 length of stamens, and have short stigmas rrecoiled over the ovary which has 3 narrow grooves formed by the 6 wings. The ovoid berries are prominently narrow-grooved. Flowers sometimes have a foul odor.

Synonyms:
 = *T. lanceolatum* S. Watson var. *rectistamineum* Gates
 = *T. rectistamineum* (Gates) St. John
 = *T. discolor* sensu Chapman
 = *T. maculatum* sensu Anderson

Cultivars:
'Eco Decorated Giant' - large maroon flowers and large brilliantly patterned leaves.

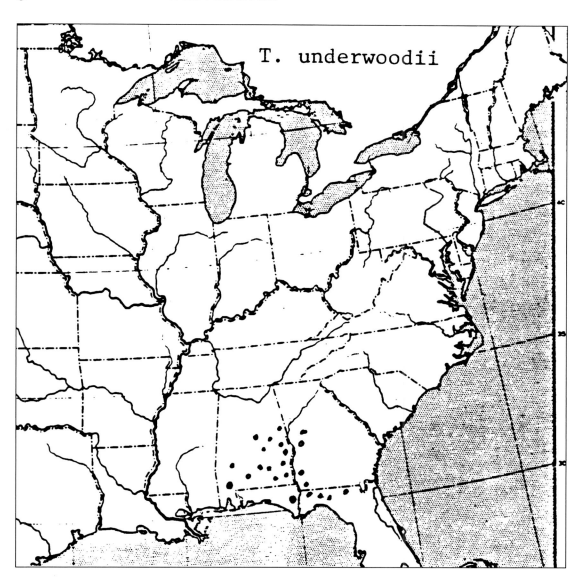

T. underwoodii

Trillium ludovicianum Harbison
"Louisiana Toadshade"

This close kin, but reduced version, of *T. decipiens* is only slightly less attractive. It probably represents the western population of a formerly more widely distributed type. The broad Mississippi River, together with the Pearl River Valley to the east, and vicissitudes in the Lower Coastal Plain have effectively long-isolated it from the eastern plants. Long, independent evolution has achieved recognizable differences, chiefly in stature. Compared to *T. decipiens*, the Louisiana toadshade has somewhat smaller rhizomes, stems to about 12 inches rather than 15 inches, leaves to about 5 inches with blunt

Trillium ludovicianum

points rather than about 6 inches with sharp points, and narrower petals about 2 1/2 rather than 3 - 4 inches long. *T. ludovicianum* petals may be all deep purple, but more commonly they are green above a purple base. Stamens are near identical in the two species: purplish, to one inch, with lateral gold anthers. Both have 6-ridged ovaries, but smaller to 12 mm. rather than 15 mm., and stigmas are thicker, pointed and divergent in *T. ludovicianum* rather than linear and recoiled as in *T. decipiens*. Capsules of *T. ludovicianum* may contain 30 to 50 seeds

Leaves of the Louisiana Toadshade often mimic the rich pattern common in *T. decipiens*:

a bright silvery blaze along the midrib, with rich marbling of near-black, light and dark green patches on each side. Flower and leaf color last an unusually long time in these two species, compared to other Trilliums. In the wild, they both come up in February and flower through March. It sometimes has a musky oder.

This is truly a Louisiana plant, largely restricted to the center of the State, except for a few populations in Mississippi, between the big river and the Pearl River, where they mingle with *T. cuneatum*. There is some indication of gene exchange in those populations.

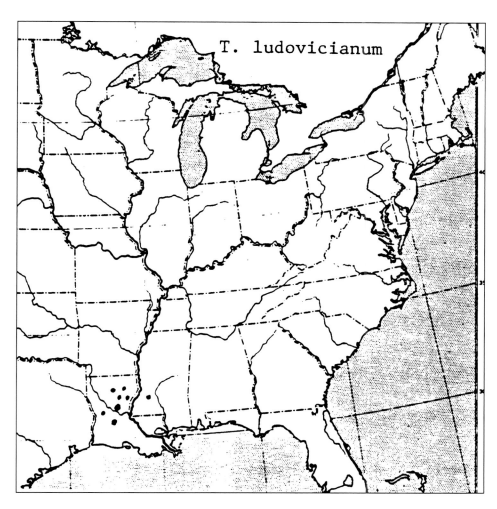

Trillium gracile Freeman
"Slender Toadshade"

This distinctive, graceful species is a westward neighbor of the Louisiana Toadshade. It is found only in sandy humus of hardwood-pine covered slopes or old flood plains on both sides of the Texas-Louisiana border. It is easily distinguished from its neighbor. Flowering in early to mid April, it is the last Southern sessile species to bloom, about 3 weeks after *T. ludovicianum*. Its leaf pattern usually consist of indiscriminate darker blotches on a gray-green background. The sessile, elliptic, blunt leaves are usually slightly drooping on smooth stems, a foot or more tall, creating a graceful effect. Narrow, purple

Trillium gracile

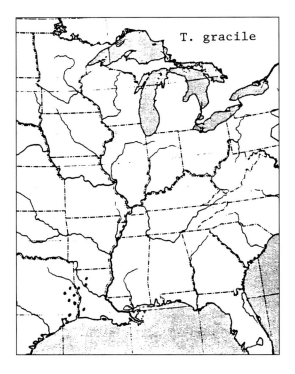

T. gracile

sepals about an inch long are spread with recurved tips. Narrow, dark-purple petals stand erect to 1 1/2 inches. Bicolor, and yellow forms occur, but rarely. Purplish stamens have yellow anthers opening inward. Small pistils have 3-angled ovaries, and stigmas with pointed recurved tips. The smooth, green, elliptic berry is often crowned with 3 pairs of prominent wings. Flowers may have a fresh mushroom odor.

Trillium decumbens Harbison

Prostrate Toadshade

Virtually everything about this handsome species is unique. Its short, prostrate stem is densely fuzzy. Its anthers look outward instead of sideways, or inward as most species do. Its leaves and floral parts disintegrate early, leaving the maturing fruit concealed in the litter. Its showy petals are somewhat divergent, and twisted. Leaves are prominently patterned dark-green borders and basal blotches on silvery green. A symmetric pattern consists of a basal heart-shape dark blotch bordered by silver and marginal dark green.

Prostrate Toadshade is an endemic found only in low mountains from northwest Georgia through northern Alabama to Tuscaloosa. It is often in humus on rocky talus slopes. It flowers from late March through April.

The rhizomes of *T. decumbens* are thick but stubby. They send out stems that thicken upward toward the leaves, and are clothed in

T. decumbens 'Eco Brite Heart' and 'Eco Spangled Silver'

short, soft hairs. They average about 6" long, spreading horizontally, so the leaves float on the litter. Broad-ovate, sessile, blunt-tip leaves are usually 3 to 4" long. Prominent sepals 1 to 2" long are often purple-stained. Large, oblanceolate, purple petals, to 3" long diverge and twist. Purplish stamens with outward facing yellow anthers can be nearly an inch long. Pistils are 1/2 as long as stamens, and deeply grooved between the 6 ovary ridges. With early disintegration of floral parts, the dark purple berries mature on bare stems in the litter. They are up to 17 x 20 mm. (WxL), and contaian up to 35 seeds.

Cultivars:

'Eco Brite Heart' - large purple flowers on symmetric leaf-pattern of silver inverted V over a dark-green basal heart.

'Eco Spangled Silver' - silver-green leaves with scattered dark-green spangles and maroon purple flowers.

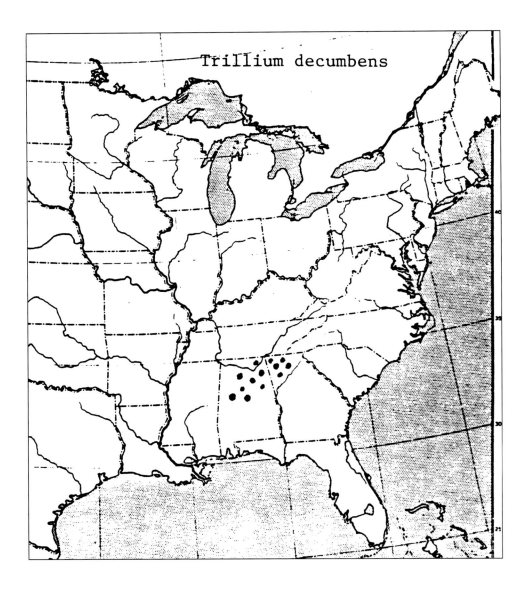

Trillium decumbens

118

Trillium reliquum Freeman
Reclining Toadshade (Relict Trillium)

This rarest of sessile Trilliums is considered, by John Freeman, to represent only the remnant populations of a formerly more widespread species, hence the name *reliquum* = relict. This is not only a reasonable conclusion, but much of the loss of territory may have occurred during the past three centuries, and still continues today. Once again, Old Man Cotton probably contributed in a major way to its demise, not only from clearing and cultivation, but also from subsequent erosion. Timber harvesting also takes a toll, but Reclining Toadshade copes fairly well, other factors being favorable. In a few instances urban development has been locally devastating. It is presently restricted to only a few sites along the Fall Line hills, from the Georgia - South Carolina border to central Georgia, and along the lower Chattahoochee Valley in southwest Georgia.

Despite this pessimistic current status, I feel that *Trillium reliquum* may have outstanding potential for gardeners. It is as durable in the garden as any southern sessile Trillium, and is no more difficult to propagate. More than this, it exhibits remarkable genetic variety throughout its limited populations.

This is the only species, other than *T. decumbens*, with a consistent reclining habit of growth, but *T. reliquum* has a smooth stem of uniform thickness, rather than pubescent and enlarging upward as *T. decumbens*.

The horizontal stems average about 6 inches in length, and arise from stubby rhizomes. The elliptic leaves to 4 inches, or slightly longer, are beautifully marbled in several colors, and many pattern-types. Narrow, spreading sepals 1 - 2 inches long are often purple stained. Elliptic petals to 2 inches long are usually dark purple, but may be bicolor green / purple or yellow. Stamens to an inch long are purple with yellow anthers turned inward. Pistils are about 1/2 as long as stamens, with 6-angled ovary constricted at summit and short stigmas.

Hopefully, several outstanding clones of *T. reliquum* will be propagated and named. It is presently unavailable to gardeners.

Varieties:
forma *luteum* - petals yellow, all flower parts lack pruple pigment.

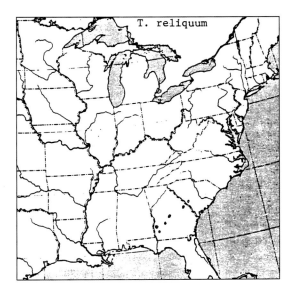

T. reliquum

Trillium reliquum

A beautiful freak with 4 leaves.

Trillium foetidissimum Freeman
"Stinking Toadshade"

East of the river, in the Mississippi Delta, in Louisiana, and southwest Mississippi is a long-overlooked sessile Trillium with a particularly foul order. It grows in old flood plain forests with several Magnolias, and on adjacent upland with Beech, Pine, Oaks, and Hickories. *Magnolia macrophylla*, *M. virginiana,* and *M. grandiflora* all occur there. Trillium foetidissimum resembles its Texas relative, *T. gracile,* but it is somewhat shorter, with larger leaves, and it flowers earlier, in late February to mid-March.

Smooth stems rise to about 10 inches from stout rhizomes. Ovate-elliptic leaves to 5 inches long are prominently marbled with irregular purple-green splotches. Spreading narrow sepals about an inch long are often

Trillium foetidissimum

T. foetidissimum

purple-stained. Narrow lanceolate petals are up to 2 inches long and purple, greenish, or yellow. Stamens, less than an inch long, are purplish with inward facing anthers. Pistils are slightly shorter than stamens, with hexagonal ovary, and rather thick, erect, pointed stigmas. On warm days the flower exudes the odor of Limburger cheese, unpleasant, but bland compared to the stench from *T. petiolatum.*

Varieties:

forma *luteum* - yellow petals, and no purple in other flower parts.

Trillium viride Beck

"Dust-Leaf Toadshade" (Green Trillium)

This relatively plain sessile Trillium may be identified by a dusted appearance of the upper leaf surfaces. Other Trilliums hve breathing pores (stomates) restricted to under-leaf surfaces, but in this species the tiny pores are sprinkled over the upper surface as well. Especially if a leaf is partially wilted, the pores are visible with the naked eye, like a dusting of silver pollen grains. The elliptic, blunt-tipped leaves, about 5 x 2 inches, or some larger, have little or no marbling. Stems may reach 15 inches. Slender green sepals, to 2 inches long, may be purple-stained at the base. Very slender, erect petals to 2 inches, or a little more, are all purple or topped with green or yellow. Stamens are up to an inch long with anthers opening inward or sideways. Pistils are shorter than stamens, with 6-angeled ovaries and erect-diverging stigmas.

122

Trillium viride

The Dust-Leaf Toadshade has a limited range on both sides of the Missouri-Illinois border. It grows in rich deciduous rocky woodland especially in calcareous valleys. It flowers mid-April to mid May and may have a cidery fragrance.

A confusing population in southern Illinois is considered, by Freeman, to be aberrant *T. viride* lacking stomates on upper leaf surfaces. Mohlenbrock considers the plants *T. cuneatum*, which represents a range extension from the nearest Kentucky site of about 100 miles.

Trillium viridescens Nutt

"Green Toadshade"

This close kin of the Dust-Leaf toadshade is frequently confused with it. This is, no doubt, the most common in cultivation, most robust, and most attractive of the two. Both have been called "Green Toadshade" but the name fits better here. Its petals are broader, often apple-green, and purple below. It may grow 20 inches tall with leaves 5 x 3 inches, or larger, and with slightly drawn-out leaaf tips. Young leaves usually have some marbling that promptly disappears. Sepals are about 2 inches long, purple-stained and somewhat broader than those of *T. viride*. Purplish stamens, about an inch long, have yellow lateral anthers, and

Trillium viridescens from Missouri.

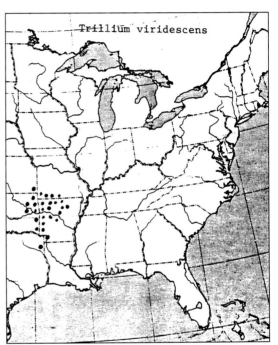

often look tangled. Pistils are about 1/2 as tall as stamens, with 6-winged ovary, and long stigmas often extending between the stamens.

Green Toadshade adapts well in most gardens and propagates readily. It flowers early April to early May with a mild spicy fragrance.

Synonyms:

= *T. stenanthes* Ref. = *T. viride* sensu Small
= *T. sessile* var. *nuttallii* S. Watson

Trillium petiolaum Pursh

"Stalk-Leaf Toadshade"

Without competition, this is the most weird of all trilliums. It exists away from all other species except the far-flung *T. ovatum*.

Unlike most sessile species, it has no leaf marbling, leaves are held up on petioles to 4 inches long, flowers are concealed near the ground, among the petioles, and they release the most horrific odor imaginable, like that of a decomposing reptile, and are pollinated by carion flies. Yet, its homeland is pristine and soul-stirring. In deep black humus, along mountain streams, at the edge of Douglas Fir Ponderosa Pine Forest, just beyond the desolate, rocky, prairie hills, it thrives in the company of Steller's Jays, Robins, Elk, and Mule Deer.

In describing *Trillium petiolatum*, Pursh compared its appearance to a clump of Plantain leaves, and this is certainly appropriate.

T. petiolatum colony in eastern Oregon.

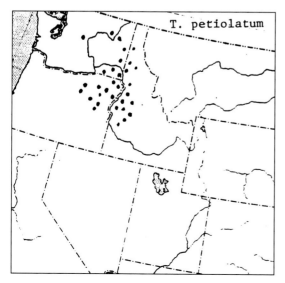

Scattered among grasses, stately *Erythronium grandiflorum*, meadow rue, false Solomon's Seal, buttercups, and violets, the clumps of round Stalk-Leaf Toadshade leaves stand out dramatically. They often occur in rather dense clumps consisting of non-flowering shoots standing erect 6 inches or more, and bearing leaves with petioles only an inch or so long, plus shoots with flowers near the ground on 2 inch stems, with 3 inch petioles, supporting near-round leaves to 5 inches long. A few shoots raise their flowers to 6 inches in crowded colonies.

Recurved sepals may be nearly 2 inches long, and narrow, erect petals reach about 2 inches. They are usually maroon purple but may be greenish. Purplish stamens with lateral yellow anthers are about an inch long. Pistils are somewhat shorter than stamens, and have 6-ridged ovaries, plus long divergent stigmas between the stamens. The ovoid berry is sharply winged. It flowers early April to late May.

The Stalk-Leaf Toadshade occurs from central Washington eastward into northern Idaho, and southward through west-central Idaho and north-east Oregon.

Efforts to correlate this Trillium with other species such as *T. sessile* and *T. recurvatum* truly stretch the imagination. Its immediate ancestors are obviously long gone, and we will probably never understand the lineage of this weird one.

A companion, *Erythronium grandiflorum*.

125

One clump of Stalk-leaf Toadshades.

A portrait of one specimen.

Trillium albidum Freeman

"Fragrant White Toadshade"

This most wide-ranging sessile Trillium on the West Coast, also has the finest fragrance, and is an outstanding garden plant. It occurs from coastal California near San Francisco, and in the Sieras to the east, then northward into central-western Oregon, southwest of Salem. It is common in shrubby thickets, forest margins, forested flood plains, and canyon slopes. It flowers mid-March to late April, depending on south to north location. In northern California to southern Oregon it flowers with *Fritillaria lanceolata*.

126   *Trillium albidum* is a large plant that can reach 2 feet in optimum sites, and the broad-ovate leaves may reach 7 inches long and wide with usually 5 veins. The spreading, green, lanceolate sepals may reach 3 inches in length, and the firm white petals may attain 4 x 1

T. albidum portrait.

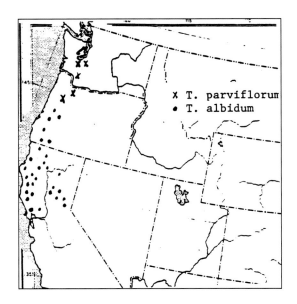

X T. parviflorum
• T. albidum

inches or more. White stamens with lateral yellow anthers may be over an inch long, and usually green pistils with 6-ridged ovaries are shorter, with nearly erect stigmas. Purple pigment may color the petal bases, stamen filaments, or pistils in some plants. Very rarely pale pink flowers occur. The large glossy leaves exhibit little or no marbling.

T. *albidum* in Josephine County, Oregon.

When air temperature exceeds 50° F., on sunny days, a rich fragrance of Tea Roses permeates the surrounding air, and carries for some distance. The release of perfume may continue for a week or more.

Like her father before her, Edith Dusek of Graham, Washington, has spent a long life studying plants native to her area. She is among those most responsible for pointing out the diversity occurring in Western sessile white trilliums defined by John Freeman as *Trillium albidum*. Victor Soukup of Cincinnati University agreed, and named the small-flowered populations in southwestern Washington, and northwestern Oregon *Trillium parviflorum*. In west-central Oregon, west of Salem, the "Little White" approach the southern large-flowered populations, and plants with intermediate characters are common there.

Edith has also called attention to the uniqueness of the trilliums in the mountains of extreme southwest Oregon. They are basically like typical *T. albidum*, but their petals are yellow to cream, not white, and there is no trace of purple in any flower parts. Flowering is delayed to late May rather than April as in other members of this complex. In addition, anthers of the upland plants open inward rather than laterally as in their kin. Fruits of typical *T. albidum* are dull green and prominently 6-ridged. Those of *T. parviflorum* are glossy, maroon, and round with ridges, if any, restricted to the top. The upland plants have stiffly erect stigmas, and small, round, cream and green, thin-skinned fruits, devoid of ridges. Edith calls them "Trillium confusum".

Trillium parviflorum Soukup
"Little White Toadshade"

This close kin of *T. albidum* earns its botanical name when compared to its big sister, but compared to many eastern Toadshades, it is quite husky. Its sturdy stems, about a foot tall, bear broad-ovate leaves to 5 x 3 inches, with 3 veins, and little or no marbling. Spreading, lanceolate sepals are little more than an inch long. White, erect petals are narrow, and up to 2 inches long, about 1/2 the maximum of *T. albidum*. White stamens with lateral yellow anthers are up to 3/4 inch long. Greenish pistils are about 1/2 the length of stamens, and stigmas are near erect. Fruit are usually dark maroon, glossy, elliptic, with persistent stigmas, but no ridges.

T. parviflorum portrait.

T. parviflorum with Mahonia, Wolfberry and Vancouveria in Washington.

Little White Toadshade is frequently found among Wolfberry (Symphoricarpos), or other small shrubs, under oaks or other deciduous trees. Sometimes it is in mixed forest with Maples, Douglas Fir and other conifers, plus *Trillium ovatum*. It has a subtle but pleasant fraagrance suggesting clove-scented soap, not at all like the rich Tea Rose fragrance of *T. albidum*. It is known only from woodlands south of Tacoma, Washington, southward beyond Portland to Polk County, west of Salem. It meets *T. albidum* there, where intergrades may occur.

Where *T. parviflorum* occurs, it is usually in widely-scattered congested groups. It seems not to occur in expansive colonies.

Trillium angustipetalum (Torrey) Freeman
"Slender-Petal Toadshade"

This robust Trillium with very slender petals probably had a rather extensive range along our Western Coastal region prior to recent geologic and climatic changes in the area. Today it is found only in the interior of California along the Sierras from Placer County southward, and along the coast to the south in the Santa Lucia Range. It grows on slopes in montaine conifer forest and chaparral. Site elevations vary from 1000 meters in the Sierras to 60 - 200 m. on the coast.

T. angustipetalum in Dusek garden in Washington State.

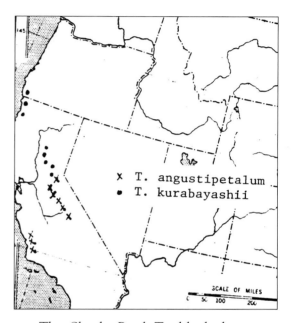

× T. angustipetalum
• T. kurabayashii

SCALE OF MILES

129

The Slender-Petal Toadshade has stout rihizomes that send up stems to 20 inches with broad ovate leaves, to 8 inches or more long, on petioles to an inch long. The leaves are usually inconspicuously marbled. Slender, spreading sepals are about 2 inches long. The very slender purple petals are up to 4 inches long and little over 1/4 inch wide. Purplish stamens about 3/4 inch long have inturned yellow anthers. Pistils are purple, about as long as stamens, and ovaries are 6-angled or winged. The stigmas are thick and erect. Berries have sharp anges and persistent fleshy stigmas.

Flowering occurs form mid-March in the south to late-May in the Sierras. The fragrance is somewhat like nutmeg.

T. kurabayashii 'Eco Klamath Gold'

Trillium kurabayashii Freeman
"Western Whippoorwill Toadshade"

This is the nearest equivalent in the West to eastern *T. cuneatum*. Its name honors Dr. Masataka Kurabayashi, a Japanese scientist who contributed greatly to our knowledge of West American Trilliums, as well as those of his homeland. *T. kurabayashii* has a very limited, split range. It grows between 300 and 1000 meters in the Sierras of Placer and Butte Counties, California. To the northwest, in the coastal mountains, it is found between 30 to 150 meters from Humboldt County, California into Curry County, Oregon. It grows most luxuriantly in deep black humus in thickets at edges of fields, edges of Redwood Forest, or in mixed deciduous-evergreen woodland.

Western Whippoorwill Toadshade has stout rhizomes, like its eastern counterpart, and produces stout stems to 18 inches. The broad leaves are up to 7 inches long, and nearly as broad, without petioles. It is, generally, more robust than *T. cuneatum*, and leaf marbling is more subdued, lacking the rich variety of contrasty patterns found in its eastern kin. Rather large, spreading sepals to 3 inches long are often purple stained. Erect petals to 5 inches long, and an inch wide are usually maroon purple, but may be bronze or yellow. Stamens to an inch long are purple with in-facing yellow anthers. Purple pistils are slightly shorter than stamens. Ovaries are hexagonal in outline, and stigmas are thick, erect, and pointed. Ovoid berries are smooth, without ridges, and usually purple, with

T. *kurabayashii* in
Humbolt County, California.

persistent stigmas. Flowers may have a nutmeg fragrance, but some have a strong citronella odor.

Cultivars:

'Eco Klamath Gold' - large, clear yellow petals, light green sepals, stamens with yellow anthers on purplish connectives. Leaves are marbled light green. From Humboldt County, California.

Trillium chloropetalum (Torrey) Howell
"California Giant Toadshade"

Restricted to the San Francisco Bay area of California is a seemingly, hopelessly mixed up population of sessile Trilliums. In addition to the richly perfumed, white-eyed white *T. albidum* approaching from the north, are various dark-eyed purple, green, yellow, white or bicolored, fragrant or scentless plants. Many names have been applied to the various extremes of the complex, but John Freeman has packaged them into two taxa in the single species *T. chloropetalum*. All have certain features in common: Anthers open inward. Pistils, and usually stamens, are purple. Stamens are about twice as long as pistils.

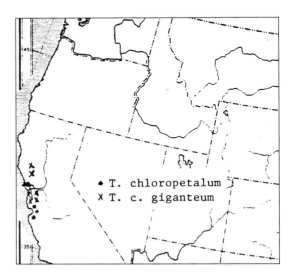

● T. chloropetalum
X T. c. giganteum

132

T. chloropetalum

Trilliuim chloropetalum giganteum at Royal Botanic Garden in Edenburgh.

Fragrance is pleasant rose-like, when present. Plants are tall, to 2 feet or more, with broad, sessile leaves, to 7 inches or more, and usually have some dark marbling.

The present diverse population most likely arose in past geologic time from a more uniform, wider-ranging population. Drastic topographic changes have occurred in the area during the past 10 to 20 million years, undoubtedly isolating fragments of the population which evolved independently. In more recent time, the segragates that survived advanced on the most agreeable habitat, and today mingle only in the Bay area. An outstanding display of plant pigments is found among them. For a detailed discussion of these refer to the chapter on "Visible Features - Plant Coloration".

Recognizing a genetic color segregation factor in the Bay Area Trilliums, John Freeman has divided them into two varieties. The plants behaving like most other sessile Trilliums he has named: *Trillium chloropetalum* var. *chloropetalum* with flowers ranging from clear yellow through light green, bronze, bicolor, to deep purple. Leaf color may vary correspondingly from light green with subdued marbling to dark green with bold purplish marbling.

A very dark form also in the
Royal Botanic Garden.

Synonyms:

T. sessile var. *chloropetalum* Torrey
T. sessile var. *californicum* S Watson
T. giganteum (Hook. & Arn.)
Heller var. *Chloropetalum* (Torrey) Gates

This variety occurs north of the Bay in Marin and Sonoma Counties, and south of the Bay in the Santa Lucia Range from Monterey to San Mateo Counties.

A variant that retains no yellow pigment in its petals he has named:
T. chloropetalum var. *giganteum*
(Hook. & Arn.) Munz

In this variety, petals may be all white, pink, bright red-purple, or various intermediate combinations, some uniquely attractive. Yellowish and greenish purple petals are not characteristic of this variety. Even the white-flowered individuals have purple pistils and some purple in the stamens. One outstanding selection has bright pink petals that redden toward the base.

Synonyms:

T. sessile var. *giganteum* Hook. & Arn
T. giganteum (Hook. & Arn.) Heller
T. sessile var. *rubrum* Hort. ex Bailey
T. sessile var. *angustipetalum* sensu
S. Watson

This variety occurs farther north in Lake and Napa Counties, as well as east and south of the Bay in Santa Cruz and Contra Costa Mountains.

Christoph Ruby of Hof, Germany studied the Trilliums in the mountains east of San Francisco and found populations with all color forms of *T. chloropetalum* intermingled, and therefore questions the usefulness of separating varieties.

134

CHAPTER 9

TRILLIUMS IN THE GARDEN

Fortunately the array of Trilliums is sufficiently diverse to tickle the whimsy of most temperate region gardeners, and to offer plants for a variety of garden habitats. All woodland shade gardens that satisfy hostas and ferns, are, by definition, desirable sties for many Trilliums. We must not conclude, however, that if you can grow one species, you can grow them all. The most wide-ranging Eastern American species are among the most easily satisfied in the garden, but a few generalizations seem to apply:

West Coast species are not easily satisfied in the East, and many Eastern species flounder in the West.

Trillium undulatum is a case unto itself, and is not suitable to gardens outside its range of occurrence.

Time of flowering may change considerably, and in unpredictable ways, in northward or southward transplanting.

Earliest flowering varieties hold flowers longest.

Most species can tolerate flooding during Spring flowering period, but many prefer a dry, Summer-dormant period.

Despite some deep set tubers in the wild, all species seem to prefer shallow rooting in the garden. Spring shoot buds are usually just beneath the forest litter.

Virtually all wild trilliums are found in deep, commonly black, humus or sandy humus, even on rocky slopes.

If leaf litter is thick in woodland gardens, seedling survival can be enhanced by careful, light raking in early Spring (February in Georgia).

Premature colapse of foliage is usually due to Botrytis infection associated with abnormally warm-humid Spring weather, and is not easily treatable.

Healthy Trilliums normally hold firm foliage until fruits are near-tipe. Immature, or unpollinated plants may ripen off earlier.

Trilliums in sunny sites exhibit, smaller, thicker, often curled leaves, and ripen earlier.

While upland species (*T. catesbaei, grandiflorum, erectum*) can thrive in constantly moist soil, they are accustomed to Summer drought periods. Flood plain species such as *T. rugelii, cernuum,* and *cuneatum* also occur in uplands but usually in rich, moist, high rainfall sites, and thrive best in gardens where summer moisture is maintained. Actually, soil moisture may be more critical than generally realized for some species. The dainty western *Trillium rivale* does not have a good record of survival in the East. In its home in Northern California and the Siskiyous of Oregon its roots are emersed in cool fresh seepage water in spring when flowering, even though they appear to be growing on slopes among rocks. Eastern gardens with seepage sites, not stagnant bogs, please these little charmers. Most Western Trilliums perform better in the east when soil moisture is maintained through the summer. Short of a stagnant bog site, it is virtually impossible to overwater flowering Trilliums.

Since Trilliums are usually growing in deep humus soils, fertility is seldom a problem. Their soils are always acid, but species like *T. nivale* and *recurvtaum* appreciate dolomite chips blended into the soil. Where rainfall exceeds 40 inches per year (Eco-Gardens = 50 inches) we recommend a top dressing of balanced fertilizer and powdered dolomite following planting. This is repeated thereafter, only if pale foliage indicates a nutrition problem. Where rainfall is less, dolomite is not advised.

With care, Trilliums may be transplanted successfully any time the ground is not frozen, but July through September is ideal. There is less risk to rhizome injury if they are dug just before foliage has ripened off. Soil should be moist when digging, to reduce risk of breaking rhizomes when hard soil cracks open. Any blend of organic compost and sand is likely to satisfy most species at planting time.

Even under ideal conditions, Trilliums seldom maintain foliage longer than 3-4 months. Insect damage during that time is seldom serious, although caterpillar browsers may reduce vigor by consuming a major part of some leaves. Mites can cause premature ripening, and grasshoppers or katy-dids sometimes feed on fruits.

Voles occasionally damage some rhizomes, although Trilliums seem not to be high on their gourmet list. Aside from browsing by deer, the greatest threat to Trillium well-being

may be botrytis rot. Healthy plants suddenly dvelop translucent spots on the foliage. These expand rapidly, and shreds of fungus with beaded white reproductive bodies may appear on the stem. The parasite may not spread to the rhizome, or damage it directly, but premature total collapse of photosynthetic tissue reduces reserves. This can be devastating if repeated in successive years. At Eco-Gardens, *Trillium maculatum* and *T. vaseyi* are most often attacked. Strangely, the former is a very early species, and the latter is usually last to bloom. In cool dry Springs botrytis is seldom seen. No treatment is effective once the disease is observed, but a preventive fungicide spray may be justified on particulary susceptible plants.

At Eco-Gardens in Georgia, flowering season for Trilliums begins with *T. underwoodii* in late February and ends with *T. vaseyi* in late April to early May. With excepion of *T. pusillum*, all of the earliest flowering are Southern sessile species. This sequential patten does not follow with northward transplanting. In Michigan (zone5) *T. underwoodii* goes from first to last, not flowering until mid-May, if at all. Surprisingly, this species usually flowers about two weeks later in its North Florida habitat (250 miles south) than at Eco-Gardens. An interesting soil temperature effect must be at work. In general, late blooming species exhibit little response to latitude.

Trillium vaseyi, erectum, flexipes, and *grandiflorum* are usually flowering within 10 days of each other in Northern and Southern gardens. Species with large latitudinal or altitudenal ranges may exhibit considerable ranges in flowering time. Most clones of Trillium cuneatum selected from local populations, near Eco-Gardens at approximately 1000 feet elevation, flower in late March, but cultivar, 'Eco Dappled Lemon', from 2500 feet in North Georgia flowers two weeks later in mid April. The precise date that a plant becomes active in Spring, and the date flowers are ready for pollination can vary 10 days plus or minus, from one year to the next, depending on climatic cycles, but later flowering species show least variation.

In the following chart, data for several years are averaged, so as to present the most simple comparison of species as to Spring awakening, and flower maturity in Northern and Southern gardens.

Comparative Phenology for Trillium Species

At Two Different Locations

Location A = Eco-Gardens, Atlanta, Georgia   Zone 7/8 33° N.
Location B = Mt. Cuba & vicinity, Delaware   Zone 6/7 40° N.

Dates are averages of several observations from 1990 to 95, and are intended primarily for sequential and latitudinal comparison.

Firts date = average date of appearance above ground.
Second date = average date of flowers with ripe pollen.

	A		B	
Trillium albidum	3/15	4/1		
Trillium catesbaei	4/1	4/15	4/18	5/5
Trillium cernuum	4/1	4/15	4/12	5/1
Trillium cuneatum, local	3/10	3/25	3/25	4/20
Trillium cuneatum Mississippi	2/15	3/1		
T.c. 'Eco Dappled Lemon'	4/1	4/15		
Trillium decipiens	2/10	3/10	3/22	4/25
Trillium decumbens	2/20	3/20	3/15	4/20
Trillium discolor	3/15	4/10	4/15	5/10
Trillium erectum	3/25	4/5	4/5	4/15
Trillium flexipes	4/1	4/15	4/15	5/1
Trillium gracile	2/15	4/5		
Trillium grandiflorum	4/1	4/10	4/10	4/20
Trillium kamtschaticum	3/25	4/5		
Trillium kurabayashii	3/12	4/1		

Trillium lancifolium	3/15	4/1	3/25	5/11
Trillium ludovicianum	2/10	3/15		
Trillium luteum	3/25	4/1	4/4	4/18
Trillium maculatum	2/10	3/15		
Trillium nivale	3/15	4/1		
Trillium ovatum	3/25	4/5		
Trillium parviflorum	3/15	4/5		
Trillium persistens	4/1	4/15		
Trillium petiolatum	3/25	4/5		
T. pusillum virginianum	3/1	3/18	4/4	4/20
Trillium ozarkanum	3/15	4/1		
Trillium recurvatum	3/25	4/15	4/10	5/1
Trillium reliquum	2/20	3/20		
Trillium rivale	3/15	4/5		
Trillium rugelii	3/25	4/15		
Trillium sessile	3/5	3/25	3/22	4/20
Trillium simile	4/1	4/12		
Trillium stamineum	3/15	4/5	4/1	5/1
Trillium sulcatum	3/30	4/10	4/10	4/20
Trillium underwoodii	1/20	3/1	5/1*	5/15
Trillium vaseyi	4/10	5/1	4/15	5/5
Trillium viride	3/20	4/10		
Trillium viridescens	3/15	4/10	4/5	4/25
Paris polyphylla	5/15	6/1		

139

* Michigan, L. Nordstrom

CHAPTER 10

TRILLIUM PROPAGATION - SEEDS

Much of what has been written on propagation of Trilliums has been over-generalized, over-complicated, over-simplified, or under-verified. It is commonly stated that Trillium seeds have a double-dormancy, so that the first leaf doe not appear above ground until the second Spring after Summer planting of fresh seeds. It is also stated that Trilliums require at least 6 to 10 seasons of growth to produce first flowers. While both of these statements can be demonstrated, they are unnecessarily discouraging and simplistic. I have found that most seeds of a number of Trillium species germinate by the first March after outdoor July planting of fresh seeds, and many germinate by November within five months of planting. Usually a portion exhibit delayed germination until the following spring. If the seedlings receive constant moisture and fertility, and are protected from excess sunlight, they will remain active for months. *Trillium pusillum* can be brought to flowering the fourth year after planting in this manner. Dr. James McClements of Dover, Delaware reports flowers in three years from germination.

In one test, 176 of 200 *Trillium nivale* seeds planted, fresh, June 5 outdoors at Eco-Gardens germinated between November 1 and 20 of the same season, (minimum temperature was 43°F on October 17), and first leaves remained green and healthy until late the following June. Some are ready to flower after three more years of healthy growth.

In the test of *Trillium pusillum virginianum*, 28 fresh seeds were planted indoors at a constant room temperature of 70°F-75°F on June 19. By August 23, 12 had germinated, and 26 had germinated by September 10, over 90% in 83 days.

Trillium sessile seeds from a southern Ohio population tested at room temperature on June 16 gave a germination of 16 out of 20 by September 24.

Tests of *Trillium catesbaei* resulted in most seeds beginning germination the same fall as ripened, but under garden conditions, the first leaf is not green and exposed until March or April.

Seeds of *Trillium kurabayashii* and *T. chloropetalum* planted outdoors produced no first leaves until second Spring after planting. These have not been retested.

At Eco-Garden in Georgia most Trilliums ripen their seeds in June to early July. If washed and planted promptly, most species give 5-90% germination during the first 120 days without experiencing temperatures below 45°F. Light exposure is not a factor. *Trillium grandiflorum* is certainly the most tested of all species, and is the source of most double-dormancy conclusions. Unquestionably, this and other northern species, at least partially, follow this life-history pattern in nature, but numerous variables may alter the behavior. If *T. grandiflorum* seeds are harvested as soon as berries begin to soften, thoroughly washed, promptly planted, and maintained at an average 70°F temperature, many will

140

germinate during the first 120 days, and most of the remainder germinate after normal winter exposure.

By examining field conditions in Trillium woodlands we soon discover that these plants have adapted to *less than ideal* conditions, but are not necessarily dependent on them. When seeds are ripe, they are either promptly carried off by ants, or drop as a blob on the dry litter beneath the parent. In either case, they are likely to be too dry to germinate until fall rains return. By then, temperatures drop below freezing, and everything is on "Hold" until spring when germination may initiate, but returns to "Hold" for the dry summer. The first above ground leaf may then appear with rains of fall or the following spring. The fact that not all seeds from a berry march to the same drummer is an advantage in survival, even though it guarantees lack of uniformity in seed beds.

If commercial production is the goal, a simple principle must prevail: Maintain optimum vigor as long as possible. This entails near neutral, porous, sandy humus, constant moisture, liquid fertilizing during active period, and strong but filtered light. Protection from browsing by insects, slugs, or mammals is vital. While some smaller species can be brought to flower in four years, most larger species require 5 or 6 years. In view of this investment in time, it makes sense to be selective in quality of parents from which to collect seeds. A tedious process? Yes! But thick of it as an assembly-line requiring about 4 years start-up. By planting yearly, a harvest is ready each year thereafter.

It should come as no surprise to discover that, in general, seeds of Trilliums have evolved no special resistance to drought or prolonged drying. They develop in moist berries, in the shade, in mesic woodlands, and have no adaptations for long-range migration. They must tolerate semi-arid conditions in the litter of Summer woodlands, but occasional rain, and frequent dew prevent complete desiccation. Most species can tolerate room-temperature, dry-air storage for 2 or 3 months, but viability drops off rapidly thereafter. A few species are more resistant. Some *T. stamineum*, *T. nivale*, and *T. viridescens* collections have yielded fair germination after six months of dry storage. *T. rivale* has yielded good germination after 8 months of dry storage, but 12 month old seed failed to germinate. Seeds of some species may remain viable for 12 months refrigerated at 40 F and kept moist, but germination may occur during refrigeration.

Work by Norman Deno in Pennsylvania, and others, indicates that germination of seeds of some Trilliums may be facilitated by gibberelins. Under some circumstances this may well be true, but it is certainly not a universal prerequisite. We have germinated many Trillium seeds, in minimal time, on sterile paper towels, in a moist chamber, after sterilizing the seeds.

From the above evidence it is safe to conclude that not all Trilliums exhibit the same germination behavior in regard to timing. There is also little evidence of a temperature effect triggering initiation of germination, although the embryo development rate is obviously controlled by temperature.

Trillium decipiens, a southern sessile species from southwest Georgia, strangely illustrates delayed germination even though it experiences only brief subfreezing temperatures in nature. Fresh seeds planted in July, in soil, in a container under mesh, in the garden, average only 5-10% germination the next March, about 75% germinated a year later. An additional 10% may germinate the third year. Sterilized seeds at a constant room temperature (70°F), on damp paper towels, in a covered plastic box, in diffuse light, behave in the same manner, except that cotyledons expand by January instead of March of successive years. When sterile damp seeds are refrigerated at 40°F. from November through January the pattern persists, with most seeds germinating in February of the second cycle, and a few in the first and third cycles.

By contrast, another southern sessile species from east Texas, *Trillium gracile*, yields about 50% germination in four months, at room temperature, in a plastic box. If transferred to soil in a container at room temperature, the cotyledons expand fully in the next 2 or 3 months. Most of the remaining seeds germinate in the Fall of that year.

Obviously, each species should be dealt with independently when propagating by seed, but it would be wise to assume that germination may occur within eight months when fresh seeds are planted in July, and if constant temperature is maintained, germination may occur in five months or less. The exceptions will mostly germinate in about 20 months. There is usually little difference in vigor between short-term and long-term seedlings. As with most plants, occasionally albinism is encountered. These chlorophyll-free white seedlings have no future once their initial food reserves are exhausted. Most of their green siblings are carriers of this recessive gene, so it would be wise to avoid collecting seeds from them or their parents in the future.

It is conceivable that, as commercial production of Trilliums from seed increases, some faster maturing clones may be selected, as will clones of superior garden worthiness. Richard Fraser at Thimble Farm on Salt Spring Island, British Columbia, is to be commended for his willingness, and successes in working with Trillium seedlings.

VEGETATIVE PROPAGATION

We may look to experience from the wild for information on Trillium propagation. A few species exhibit very efficient natural vegetative propagation that is readily utilized. *Trillium pusillum virginianum* is a prime example. It grows from slender, horizontal, rapidly-branching, white rhizomes. With annual lifting, separating, and replanting in loose compost, at least a 3-fold increase per year may be attained. This species does not occur as scattered individuals in the wild, but rather, in dense colonies. The sessile-flowered *T. lancifolium* behaves similarly.

Species with stout rhizomes vary considerably in their propensity to produce multiple shoots, both between species and between individuals. A robust *T. cuneatum* plant has remained undisturbed in Eco-Gardens more than 16 years with no natural vegetative reproduction. During its 12th to 16th years it consistently produced 2 flowering shoots from its single terminal rhizome bud, but no rhizome divisions have formed. By the propagation method to be described, at least 100 to 150 offspring could have been produced in that period of time. Other *T. cuneatum* clones ('Eco Silver Tiara' and 'Eco Spectacular' for example) have freely produced offshoots spontaneously. Since leafy flowering shoots exist for only a single season, rhizome branching, and natural propagation require initiation of lateral buds into persistent terminal rhizome buds. Rhizome branches resulting by rejuvenation from lateral buds usually require another year or two to build sufficient reserves for flowering. During that time, the young rhizome fattens with stored

142

starch, the buds enlarge, and the root system expands. This type of adjustment is also required when transplanted rhizomes are delayed in replanting.

The simplest, effective means of propagating stout rhizome Trilliums is a method of decapitation. The rhizomes are dug, and washed free of soil as soon as the tops ripen off in July or August. A sharp, thin blade is then used to cut across the rhizome behind the two year old increment. The tip with most active roots is replanted with damp Sphagnum Moss against the wound, and no other treatment. It will usually continue to grow and flower as though nothing had happened, but may be slightly smaller for a season. If the remaining stump is exceptionally large (more than twice as long as thick), it may be cut in half. These stumps are then set 1-2 inches deep in humus soil (with Sphagnum Peat against the wounds) for regeneration. By the following summer, from 2-8 new tubers with strong roots will have formed on each stump, and some, but not all tubers, have produced a single leaf that is now ripening off. By the second spring, healthy new shoots appear. They should be fertilized and kept moist until they ripen off. They can then be lifted, and separated from the stumps, which should be replanted for further regeneration. The young plants should be promptly planted out, and usually bloom the second spring, four years after the rhizome was cut, but sometimes in three years.

Numerous other accounts of vegetative propagation of Trilliums have been published Virtually all are more tedious than the procedure just described, and none report superior results.

One procedure involves a kind of circumcision, which may be performed with or without lifting the plant. A shallow, circular groove is cut around the rhizome, near the growing end, where upon new sprouts develop behind the circumcission.

Another proposal is a destructive form of decapitation, usually performed without lifting the plant. The terminal bud is simply removed by scooping it out. The main flowering plant is thus sacrificed in order to induce lateral sprout development. If the excising is not sufficiently radical, a following-season preformed terminal bud will take over and inhibit lateral sprouts.

Still another manipulation can be performed without lifting the plant. The soil is scraped back to expose the upper surface of the rhizome. A sharp knife tip is then used to cut a shallow, lengthwise groove back from the growing tip, with the expectation of sprouts appearing along the groove. I have no data on effectiveness of this.

All vegetative propagation techniques are based on the principal of *apical dominance*, in which hormones produced in a shoot tip diffuse backward, and inhibit lateral shoot development. By temporarily eliminating the inhibitors, undifferentiated tissue can initiate new buds, which develop into new plants. By adding chemical stimulants to the process Margery Edgren of Woodside, California worked with *T. chloropetalum* to attempt to speed the process. She treated Trillium stumps with cytokinin hormone to induce sprout initiation. She then treated these with giberellic acid to speed development. She attempted to enhance development further by alternating 16 hour light exposure at room temperature, with 8 hour dark in a refrigerator, each day. Apparently tiny buds with small strip leaves developed and ripened off in seven months or so, where upon the clump was rinsed and refrigerated for 3 months. After repotting, and returning to alternating

T. underwoodii propagation photo taken March, 1992 in the garden showing
three 3-year old seedlings at left, and 7 new vegetative offshoots
from a rhizome segment removed from plant at the right.

The same plant and propagating segment lifted and photographed June, 1992.
Some of these young plants flowered March, 1994.

warm light, and cold dark until new growth ripened, refrigeration was repeated for 3 months. After repeating the cycles for 7 seasons, some tubers had attained a length of about 1 inch but none had yet flowered. The best case produced 11 plants from a treated stump.

By comparison, a single untreated stump of T. *underwoodii* produced 7 sprouts that were removed 20 months later. Four of these flowered 20 months later, three years and four months after cutting. In addition, the replanted stump produced another 4 tubers the next year, for a total of 11 the same as the chemically, temperature, and light manipulated T. *chloropetalum*. My work with T. *underwoodii* has been repeated many times, with many species, with similar results, all under uncontrolled, seasonal, outdoor conditions, except to insure moisture, and supplement fertility. There may be potential benefit in numbers from use of cytokinin stimulation, but the food reserves in the Trillium stumps are finite, and the number of robust sprouts that can be produced is thereby limited. Since time is a vital factor, producing vegetative sprouts no more advanced than seedlings has limited value unless we can somehow reduce the usual time to flowering.

Selecting for naturally fast-propagating clones holds promise. Dr. Lighty's T. *grandiflorum* 'Quicksilver' is a registered example. Henning von Schmeling's prolific T. *vaseyi* is another.

MICROPROPAGATION

Commercial horticulture has, in recent time, come to rely heavily on tissue culture laboratories to furnish limitless quantities of slow propagating plants. We need only consider the tremendous explosion of Hosta gardens to observe the results. If similar results could be achieved with Trilliums, it would be a great boon. A number of researchers have, and are making the effort, but, to this time, Trilliums are not commercially available from tissue culture.

Randy Burr of Mount Vernon, Washington has been able to get *Trillium luteum* into sterile culture, but has not proceeded to commercial production. He began with young shoots prior to their emergence from protective sheaths. Calluses formed and produced leafy tubers. These gave rise to abundant bulblets, but there was little progress toward mature plants.

In 1986, Valerie Pence and Victor Soukup reported on their research on Trillium micropropagation. They worked with portions of young leaves, ovules, and portions of rhizomes from 19 species. These included *Trillium albidum, cernuum, decipiens, decumbens, discolor, erectum, flexipes, gracile, grandiflorum, kurabayashii, ludovicianum, luteum, maculatum, nivale, pusillum, rugelii, simile, underwoodii,* and *viridescens*. Calluses that went on to produce young plants were achieved in three species: T. *decipiens, flexipes,* and *grandiflorum*, all from leaf buds. Embryo-like structures that produced young plants developed from sections of 1/2 grown leaves of T. *pusillum*. In a few species, some callus that did not differentiate occurred. Bacterial and fungal contamination occurred in some cultures, and regenerated young plants were able to continue growth for weeks despite contamination. Only *Trillium decipiens* gave commercially encouraging results. Plants with 3 leaves were obtained in less than two years. By starting new cultures from regenerated plants, it was possible to produce approximately 500 plants in 4 years from two initial explants.

Work with Trilliums in tissue laboratories continues, and in addition to promising a brighter future for gardeners and conservationists, a better understanding of these plants is sure to result. The work of Ron Gagliardo at the Atlanta Botanical Garden is particularly encouraging. Ron is working with seeds and plant portions. After preliminary tests, he has chosen young shoots prior to emerging from basal sheaths as preferred material for cultivar propagation. The very young stem is cut below the leaves, the flower bud (if present) is cut away, and outer portions of leaves are cut away. The remaining segment is then sterilized and stuck into sterile culture gel in a small glass container under fluorescent lighting at about 70°F. Substantial calluses are usually formed in 3 to 4 months, and differentiation into tuberous rhizomes from slender proliferation's soon follows. Within 12 months after preparation, new rhizomes as large as 3-year-old seedlings can develop. Surprisingly, strong, contractile, adventitious roots are sometimes already pushing through the gel by then. This demonstrates the inherent nature of these roots as independent of environmental factors.

The medium producing these results is notably simple. The only organic food is sucrose sugar in a standard solution of inorganic salts and trace elements, with small amounts of thiamin and inositol. No giberellin, but small amounts of naphthalene acetic acid and cytokinins are added. Sterilized fresh seeds have given comparable results on this medium. Germination usually begins within 4 months at 70°F under fluorescent lights. This is approximately the behavior that I have observed with many Trillium species in soil culture, or when placed on damp toweling in a covered plastic box at room temperature. Seeds not germinating in 4 months may wait 12 months longer to germinate, whether refrigerated or left at room temperature. An amazing acceleration of seedling development can proceed in the culture medium. Fifteen months after planting, some *Trillium cuneatum* seedlings produced shoots with 3 leaves from rhizomes the size of normal 3-year-old seedlings.

These successes are very gratifying, but considerable devotion and hard work still is required to bring the produce to market. Gardeners far and wide will be indebted to these conscientious workers. Despite the promise of this work, it can augment, but not replace normal soil seedling production, and rhizome segment propagation.

Trillium grandiflorum rhizome prior to breaking dormancy, and a rhizome from which twin shoots have been removed and trimmed for micropropagation. Flower buds and outer leaf portions have been cut away.

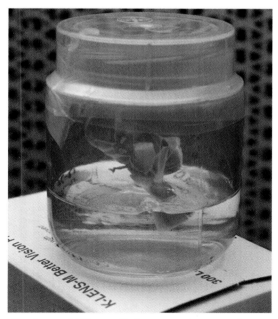

Fresh-cut *Trillium albidum* in culture medium.

Mass of young *T. grandflorum* plants nearly ready to plant out. Produced from shoot segment placed in culture 12 months earlier.

12-month-old cultures:
Left: A husky young *T. luteum* plant already producing contractile roots.
Right: Vigorous young *T. ozarkanum* plants.

A *T. cuneatum* seed-coat still attached to its cotyledon. The embryo has produced a rhizome and young shoot, plus a calus mass and abundant roots after 14 months in culture.

148

CHAPTER 11

TRILLIUM MIGRATION

Trilliums thrive and compete successfully only in certain habitats. How have they reached and spread thru those habitats? The various species sort themselves between mature flood-plain woods, upland woods, and rocky, mountain slopes. In flood plains, and along stream banks,, heavy Spring rains, and flooding can carry germinating seeds some distance downstream. In the mountains, land slides can bring the plants to lower levels, but how do they ascend? Actually, there are few means by which Trilliums can migrate between isolated suitable habitats. In Eastern North America this was previously no problem, because deciduous forests were continuous from the Atlantic to the Mississippi. One means of travel is a mixed blessing. Browsing animals, chiefly White-tail Deer in the east, and Elk and Mule Deer in the west, can transport seeds for miles in their gut. This, of course, presupposes that the animals do their browsing at the right time in June or July when fruits are ripening. With modest deer populations this is a reasonable likelihood. With present excessive populatons, few unprotected plants survive that long through the Spring.

There remains a possibility that some Trillium seed dispersal is accomplished by birds. At least the Himalayan *Trillium govanianum* and the American *T. undulatum* have modest-size, smooth, red, berry fruits, conceivably attractive to birds. Since our observations reveal that most *T. undulatum* fruits mature on the plants, and birds have not been observed plucking them, we conclude that bird dissemination is of little consequence. Apparently, long-range *Trillium* migration is now virtually non-existent. This largely restricts migration to within stable communities, and limits genetic interchange.

Within communities, ants are unquestionably the usual dispersal agents for Trilliums. Trillium fruits are quite large fleshy berries that either disintegrate in place or drop intact to the ground. In either case, the seeds and young plants remain in immediate competition with the parent plant. Far-ranging ants, in search of food, usually preclude this. They efficiently home-in on the protein-rich aril collar of the large, but portable seeds, and carry them to their dens. There they consume the aril and discard the seeds. I have observed ants carrying *Trillium cuneatum* and *T. catesbaei* seeds for at least 18 feet. It is reasonable to assume that Trillium seeds can be thus dispersed at least 20 feet in any direction from flowering clumps each year. In North Georgia, at least some seedlings can flower the fifth year after disperal. This would extrapolate into an average possible migration rate of 4 feet per year, or 400 feet per century - not a rapid process, but constant. This process does more to insure full utilization of a given habitat than to achieve expansion of territory. It also helps to intersperse the genetic variants in a population.

If a gardener attempts to plant fresh Trillium seeds outdoors, he soon discovers how efficient ants can be. Unless covered with soil immediately, the seeds will be observed marching from the furrow about as fast as they are placed there. Apparently Trilliums and ants have been evolutionary partners for millenia.

149

CHAPTER 12

HYBRIDS AND HYBRIDIZATION

We have already dealt with hybridization from several viewpoints, but additional features need to be considered. Hybrids may result from the combining of sperm and egg between two individuals of distinctly different genetic constitution. They may be members of a single species, or two different species, or so different that they have been classed in different genera. As a general rule, the greater the difference between individuals, the lesser the likelihood of successful hybridization. Hybrids between individuals of different genera occur, but are rare. No intergeneric hybrids involving Trilliums are known.

Certain generalizations carried over from controlled plant breeding work need to be qualified when dealing with wild plants. The principle of "Hybrid Vigor" presupposes that both parents are products of long-term line-breeding to achieve maximum uniformity in genetic constitution. Their offspring may then benefit by an additive effect of their diverse qualities of size, fruitfulness, disease-resistance etc. While a degree of hybrid vigor may be revealed among natural hybrids, it can not be anticipated.

Further, the concept of a uniform first generation of hybrids, with a predictable segregation of kinds in the second generation from interbreeding the first offspring, assumes a genetic uniformity in the wild parents that seldom exists. Nevertheless, self-pollination in Trilliums is so common that establishing relatively-pure line-bred strains is plausible. These may then be hybridized to produce desirable new varieties of a species.

The common concept that new species often arise immediately from hybridization

between different species has minimal support in fact. Most hybrids between species in nature are dead-ends. Often they are sterile, producing no seeds, some living for years with only slow, vegetative propagation. Annuals are gone after a single year. Some are self-sterile but interfertile. These may be pollinated by their parent types, and in time their hybrid character may diffuse through the population and largely disappear. When this occurs in a small, isolated colony, the hybrids may have a greater impact, and hybrid characters may eventually dominate the population. Such populations may become recognized as distinct species. This may well be the course of origin of *Trillium sulcatum* from *T. erectum* x *T. flexipes*.

Actually, many examples in the plant world of "instant speciation" by hybrid polyploidy exist. In Japan, only three natural Trillium species are recognized: *T. kamtschaticum* (10 chromosomes), *T. tschonoskii* (20 chromosomes), and *T. apetalon* (20 chromosomes). All possible hybrid combinations of these have been observed in the wild. Virtually all of these first generation hybrids are sterile, but in those instances where allopolyploidy resulted in doubling the hybrid's 15 chromosomes to 30, the plants became fertile, self-propagating colonies recognized as distinct species. Nothing comparable has occurred among American Trilliums.

In fact, a number of American Trilliums are not suspected of fraternizing with any but their own kind. These include: *T. grandiflorum, nivale, catesbaei, discolor,* persistens, undulatum, petiolatum, decumbens, lancifolium, recurvatum, stamineum, and reliquum. Actually, natural hybrids are sufficiently rare as to be noteworthy. No hybridization between sessile and pedunculate specie has been discovered, and no garden hybrids between Western and Eastern American species have been reported, although it seems likely that some crosses could be made.

Among reputed hybrids from the wild and from gardens, are some particularly attractive plants of outstanding garden merit. At sites in western North Carolina, a group of *T. rugelii* x *T. erectum* hybrids with generous-size nodding flowers in shades of pink to rose were discovered. They are intermediate in pistil and stamen characters. The complex interbreeding in the *T. erectum-flexipes sulcatuum*-complex has been discussed under *T. sulcatum*. These species may also hybridize with *T. vaseyi* and *T. simile*, yielding puzzling specimens.

A most unexpected hybrid between *T. ovatum* and *T. rivale* has been named 'Del Norte' for the northern-most California county where it was discovered. Judging from some British Columbia plants, it appears that *T. ovatum* also hybridizes with *T. hibbersonii*.

While hybridization between Trillium species is not common, it is normal between different types of single species. This is most noteworthy among the different color forms of species like *T. erectum*. This species may occur in quite pure colonies of red, white, or yellow, as well as mixed red, white, and pinks of every shade. Where yellow colonies are near red colonies, unusual copper blends occur. A similar situation exists where yellow and purple *T. cuneatum* occur in proximity. Bronze intermediates should be expected.

To this time, planned Trillium breeding programs have been wanting. Hopefully, the present work will encourage activity in that direction. Unlimited demand for the fruits of such labors will repay the efforts.

151

Hybrids of *Trillium rugelii* x *erectum* in western North Carolina.

EPILOGUE

Perchance we may meet on woodland trails where drifts of Trilliums and singing Robins still greet the Spring. The more we walk such trails, the more familiar the plants and animals become. Eventually, without studying details, we recognize each kind at a glance, as we do old friends. Occasionally we encounter a Trillium stranger that defies placement in a recognized species. It will not be bettered or degraded by forcing it into a named category. Like a unique friend, appreciate it for its individuality, even though you speculate on how it came to be.